SIX Ingredients *or Less*

Cooking Light & Healthy

Also by Carlean Johnson

Six Ingredients or Less

Six Ingredients Or Less Chicken Cookbook

SIX Ingredients *or Less*

Cooking Light & Healthy

Carlean Johnson

CJ
BOOKS
Washington

First Printing 1992
Sixth Printing 1996

Notice: The information in this book is true to the best of our knowledge, but it is not meant to take the place of skilled professionals and the advice of your doctor. Author and publisher disclaim all liability in connection with the use of this book.

Typography and production design: Linda Hazen
Cover design by Judy Petry
Cover photo by Fred Milkie

ISBN 0-942878-03-5

C. J. Books
P.O. Box 922
Gig Harbor, WA 98335
1-800-423-7184

Acknowledgments

The Six Ingredients or Less cookbooks have become a series which would not have been possible without the help and encouragement of so many people.

My daughter, Linda, has again, been my right arm throughout the planning and designing of this book.

I would like to thank family and friends for their support and patience when we had so many deadlines to meet.Thank you, Mom, for being my biggest fan. (If my mom walks into a store and they don't have my books, she wants to know why!)

Thank you, Judy Petry, for also designing the cover for our third cookbook, even though this was a very busy time for you. I would also like to thank Mike Milkie for giving up a sunny Saturday to photograph the cover.

A special thanks to Mike O'Connor and Mike Bednarczyk at Quantum Computers for treating us like one of the "big guys." Thanks also to the people at ESHA, the publishers of our nutritional analysis softwear, "The Food Processor II."

I also want to thank the many people who have purchased my first two books. Because of your requests, this book became number three in a series.

About The Author

Carlean Johnson resides in scenic Gig Harbor in the Puget Sound area of Washington state. With the success of her first cookbook Six Ingredients or Less, came the Six Ingredients or Less Chicken Cookbook, now followed by Six Ingredients or Less Cooking Light & Healthy. With three books on the market and no writing plans for the near future, Carlean plans on spending more time with her friends, her children and her grandchildren.

Table of Contents

Introduction

Six Ingredients or Less Cooking Light & Healthy is a result of the many requests I have had from those who have my first two cookbooks. Requests have come pouring in for a Six Ingredients or Less cookbook designed for low-fat low-cholesterol cooking for today's busy lifestyles.

The object of this book is not to cut out fat and cholesterol, but to cut down on the total amount most of us eat in our daily diets. By limiting total fat to 30% of our calorie intake we are developing a healthy way of cooking for the whole family. What better gift can we give the ones we love, than a guide to healthy eating which may lead to a longer life.

Naturally we don't want to give up the foods we love - food is one of life's greatest pleasures. By counting fat grams and eating in moderation, we can still enjoy our favorite dishes as long as we are careful about how much and how often we eat them.

What is Cholesterol?

Cholesterol is a fat-like substance essential to the daily production of cell walls and hormones. It is produced naturally by the body, stored in the body tissues and circulated in the blood. Cholesterol is also produced in the body by certain foods we eat and is found in foods of animal origin (meat, milk and eggs).

Cholesterol moves through the blood in packages of fat and protein called lipoproteins. These are manufactured in the body. Two types are:

- High-Density Lipoprotein (HDL) - This is the "good" cholesterol because it appears to clear excess cholesterol from the arteries.
- Low-Density Lipoprotein (LDL) - This is often called "bad" cholesterol, because it promotes the build-up of cholesterol in the artery walls.

We need cholesterol for our bodies to function properly, but we can also have too much of it. If the amount of LDL cholesterol is too high, fatty deposits can build up on the inner walls of arteries causing the arteries to become narrower which can eventually interfere with the blood flow. The result can be a heart attack.

In addition to high blood cholesterol, smoking and high blood pressure put you at a greater risk for heart disease.

Everyone should have their cholesterol checked. Research shows the average cholesterol count of those who have suffered a heart attack is 240. The risk of having a heart attack increases dramatically with a count of 200 or more.

Depending on your medical history, age and weight, your cholesterol count should be under 200. A count of 200 to 239 is borderline and you should follow your doctors instructions. A count of 240 or above signals a red flag. DON"T WAIT! Under your doctors guidance, start immediately on bringing your cholesterol level down.

My father had his cholesterol checked in the fall of 1989. His count was 240. He had good intentions and meant to do something about it "eventually." He was in reasonably good health, was a non-smoker and exercised by walking almost daily. Unfortunately, in January of 1990, he had a fatal heart attack. Don't let this happen to you - it may be preventable.

The good news about high cholesterol is that, in many cases, it can be brought down very quickly by limiting food high in cholesterol and reducing your total fat intake. Your doctor will advise you on diet changes you need to make. If diet doesn't lower your cholesterol, medication may be recommended.

Counting Fat Grams

Most of us want the freedom to choose what we eat. Within reason and by learning more healthy ways of eating we "can" still have our cake and eat it too.

Counting fat grams has become a popular way in the 90's to limit fat in our diets and maintain healthy eating habits. If you indulge a little too much one day you can make up for it the next couple of days by balancing your fat grams. You can also do this over a period of a week. Make sure your total weekly food counts don't go over the count per day (x) seven. This allows you to occasionally indulge in a favorite food and still maintain a healthy balance.

The American Heart Association,as well as many professionals, agree that a diet of 30% fat will significantly decrease your chance of a heart attack and possibly other life-threatening diseases.

The amount of fat grams you are allowed per day is determined by the average number of calories consumed per day. Our diets should consist of no more than 30% fat grams and of that 30% no more than 10% should come from saturated fat.

Daily Fat Gram Allowance

In order to know how many fat grams you are allowed per day, you need to know what your average daily calorie intake is. By following the chart below, you can estimate your fat gram allowance which is based on 30% of the calories you normally consume per day. Cholesterol should be limited to no more than 300 mg per day unless advised otherwise by your physician.

Calories	Fat g	Sat. Fat g
1,000	33	11
1,200	40	13
1,500	50	17
1,800	60	20
2,000	66	22
2,200	73	24
2,400	80	26
2,600	86	29
2,800	93	31

Read Labels

Many food labels are misleading. Companies want us to think their products are low in fat and cholesterol when many times they aren't. Fortunately, the FDA is now doing something about this. It takes time, but in the future we will be seeing labels that will more fairly depict what we are realistically getting in the products we buy.

Read food labels carefully. Compare products and try to get the lowest fat and cholesterol counts possible and still maintain good flavor.

To figure percentages use the following formula:

- Multiply the number of fat grams by 9 and divide that number by the number of calories per serving.
- # of fat grams ÷ calories = percentage

Abbreviations Used in This Book:

Cal - calories
Pro - protein
Carb - carbohydrates
Fib - fiber
Fat - fat grams
Sat - saturated fat grams
Chol - cholesterol milligrams
Sod - sodium milligrams
g - grams
mg - miligrams
na - not available

Foods Used in This Book:

The following foods were used in this book because of their lower fat content and/or because I felt they worked best in the recipes.

Salt- a minimum of salt has been used in the recipes for added flavor. This is not a cookbook designed for persons on a sodium-restricted diet. You can choose to use as much or as little salt as you wish or eliminate altogether.

Sugar- desserts have been included in this book because very few of us choose to give up desserts completely. Desserts, cookies, etc. should be eaten in moderation and kept within your fat allowance.

Saffola- soft tub margarine was used in all the recipes calling for margarine except where stick margarine was specified.

Milk- used nonfat which is same as skim milk.

Brands Used

Best Light Mayonnaise
Kraft Light Cream Cheese Product
Egg Beaters Egg Substitute
Hunt's Thick n' Rich Barbecue Sauce
Prego Spaghetti Sauce
Frigo Truly Lite Mozzarella cheese (This brand has only 2 fat grams per ounce and works beautifully in recipes.)
Reduced Fat Cheeses - read labels carefully and experiment to find the ones you like best
Parmesan cheese, freshly grated: Can grate or purchase in deli department.
Swanson's Chicken Broth (regular strength, not condensed)
Canola oil
Olive oil
Ground Beef - 10% or less fat content
Canned Fruits - unsweetened, packed in own juice

Must Haves:

Must haves on my list are:

- 1 (8-inch) non-stick skillet
- 1 (10-inch) deep non-stick skillet
- 10-inch non-stick skillet with raised "grills" on the bottom allowing meat to set above any fat that cooks out of the food (such as hamburgers, pork chops, etc.)
- Small scale for weighing foods - digital is best
- Vegetable cooking spray
- A calorie, fat, cholesterol and sodium count guide book
- Books on cholesterol. There are a number of excellent books on the market explaining all you want to know (and maybe more) about cholesterol, fat, etc.

Good Food Choice Suggestions

Breads:

- Whole-grain
- 100% Whole Wheat
- Multi-grain
- Dark Rye
- Pumpernickel
- Pita
- Bagels
- Corn Tortillas
- Melba Toast
- Sourdough
- Sourdough rolls
- French
- Italian
- Crumpets
- English Muffins
- Bread Sticks
- Rye Crisp
- Wasa

Cereals (low or no-fat, but watch the sugar):

- Corn Flakes
- Puffed Wheat
- Grape Nuts
- Rice Chex
- Shredded Wheat
- Crispix
- Special K
- Kix
- Total
- Wheaties
- Corn Chex
- Bran Flakes
- Rice Krispies

Oils:

- Canola
- Vegetable
- Safflower
- Olive
- Peanut

Meats (we should eat more poultry and fish and limit most other meats):

- Top Round
- Eye of Round
- London Broil
- Flank Steak
- Tenderloin
- Top Sirloin
- Chicken
- Turkey
- Lean Ham
- Canadian Bacon
- Pork Loin Chop
- Lamb Loin Chop
- Lamb Leg
- Veal Cutlet
- Veal Leg

Seafood:

- Catfish
- Cod
- Halibut
- Orange Roughy
- Salmon
- Scallops
- Snapper
- Sole
- Tuna
- Clams
- Crab
- Mussels
- Scallops
- Shrimp

Examples are based on an allowance of
60 fat g & **300** cholesterol mg per day.

	FAT G	CH MG
BREAKFAST		
1 cup cereal	0	0
1/2 cup nonfat milk	0	0
2 slices whole wheat toast	2	0
1 tablespoon jam	0	0
1/2 cup strawberries	0	0
Total	**2**	**0**
LUNCH		
Special Turkey Sandwich	6	59
Fresh Fruit Cup	0	0
Total	**6**	**59**
DINNER		
Chicken Pineapple Supreme	6	82
Lemon Vermicelli Rice	3	0
Fresh Asparagus with Red Pepper	1	1
Feather Light Muffin	8	1
Salad with Romaine	10	0
Total	**28**	**84**
Total Used	**36**	**143**

You can see that you will have had a lot of food for the day, but used only 38g of your fat allowance and only 146 mg of cholesterol. You have a balance of 22 fat grams and 154 cholesterol miligrams. If you aren't dieting you could add snacks, a low-fat dessert and/or save your grams for the next day or a special occasion later in the week. If you go over you allowance for the day, you can make up for it the next day or during "that" week. Plan to balance your fat and cholesterol counts by the end of the week. As you can see, there is freedom and flexibility in counting fat grams, but you also need to keep accurate counts.

BREAKFAST	**FAT G**		**CH MG**	
6 ounces tomato juice	0		0	
Onion Omelet	2		0	
3 ounce slice lean ham	5		47	
2 Biscuits	4		0	
2 tablespoons jam	0		0	
Total	**11**		**47**	
LUNCH				
Chicken Fajitas	13		85	
Sautéed Onion and Peppers	2		0	
Choice of Fresh Fruit	0		0	
Total	**15**		**85**	
DINNER				
Meatloaf (ground beef)	14		105	
Mashed Potatoes	0		0	
2 teaspoons margarine	7		0	
Green Bean Medley	3		3	
Jello Fruit Salad	<1		0	
Whole Wheat Muffin	3		0	
Total	**28**		**108**	
Total Used		**54**		**240**

BREAKFAST	**FAT G**		**CH MG**	
1 cup cereal	0		0	
1/2 cup nonfat milk	0		0	
Blueberry Coffeecake	15		0	
Total	**15**		**0**	
LUNCH				
Potato Soup	<1		1	
Toasted French Bread	1		1	
1 teaspoon margarine	4		0	
Apple	<1		0	
Total	**7**		**2**	
DINNER				
Baked Catfish Parmesan	8		73	
Broccoli-Tomato Dish	2		3	
Rice with Pineapple	8		0	
Sourdough Roll	0		0	
1 teaspoon margarine	4		0	
Strawberry Pie	9		0	
Total	**31**		**76**	
Total Used		**53**		**78**

Breakfast	**Fat g**	**Ch mg**
Turkey Sausage Casserole	10	51
Mixed fruit (1 cup)	0	0
Quick Cinnamon Roll	2	0
Total	**12**	**51**
Lunch		
Grinder	13	53
Light Chicken Soup	3	na
Total	**16**	**53**
Dinner		
Barbecue Flank Steak	10	57
Tiny new red potatoes	0	0
1 teaspoon margarine	4	0
Green Beans Dijon	3	0
Banana Muffin	5	0
Orange Cake	7	na
Total	**29**	**57**

Total Used **57** **161**

Breakfast	**Fat g**	**Ch mg**
Swedish Pancakes (5)	5	5
2 T *Maple Syrup with Almond*	0	0
1 cup strawberries	0	0
Total	**5**	**5**
Lunch		
Ham with Mustard Glaze	5	47
Light Cheesy Potatoes	3	13
Fresh English Peas	1	0
Spinach Salad	8	10
Sourdough Roll	0	0
1 teaspoon margarine	4	0
Total	**21**	**70**
Dinner		
Ham and Lima Bean Soup (2 cups)	2	6
Jalapeño Corn Bread	10	56
Cut-up fresh vegetables	0	0
Apple-Cranberry Crisp	8	0
Total	**20**	**62**

Total Used **46** **137**

Breakfast	Fat g		Ch mg	
6 ounces orange juice	0		0	
Oatmeal with Pineapple	1		<1	
1 English Muffin	1		0	
2 teaspoons margarine	7		0	
Total	**9**		**1**	
Lunch				
½ Tortilla Pizza	8		24	
Company Romaine Salad	11		2	
Total	**19**		**26**	
Dinner				
Baked Salmon Steaks	12		56	
Potatoes with Lemon Sauce	4		0	
Three Pepper Stir-Fry	1		0	
Spinach Salad	8		10	
Angel Food Cake	0		0	
Sliced Strawberries	0		0	
Total	**25**		**66**	
Total Used		**53**		**93**

Breakfast	Fat g		Ch mg	
6 ounces pineapple juice	0		0	
Buttermilk Pancakes (3)	2		3	
2 T Maple Syrup with Almond	0		0	
2 ounces Canadian Bacon	5		33	
Total	**7**		**36**	
Lunch				
Oriental Soup	2		14	
Toasted French Bread	1		0	
2 teaspoons margarine	7		0	
Company Romaine Salad	11		2	
Total	**21**		**16**	
Dinner				
Company Pork Chops	15		104	
Candied Carrots	2		0	
Apricot Nut Rice	6		0	
Tossed Salad with Orange	9		0	
Sourdough Roll	0		0	
2 teaspoons margarine	7		0	
Total	**39**		**104**	
Total Used		**67**		**156**

Appetizers & Beverages

CREAMY FRUIT DIP

CHILL

Delicious with fresh fruit, especially strawberries and bananas.

1 (8-ounce) container Light cream cheese product, softened
1 (7-ounce) jar marshmallow creme
1 orange (you will need 3 tablespoons orange juice and 1 teaspoon orange peel)

In mixer bowl, beat cream cheese until smooth. Add marshmallow creme; beat until smooth. Add juice and peel. Chill until ready to serve. Makes 2 cups.

Per tablespoon:

CAL	PRO	CARB	FIB	FAT	SAT	CHOL	SOD
35	<1g	6g	0g	1g	<1g	3mg	44mg

POPPY SEED-YOGURT DIP

CHILL

Use as a dip with fresh fruit. Can make day ahead.

1 (8-ounce) carton lowfat lemon yogurt
1/2 teaspoon fresh lemon peel
1/2 teaspoon poppy seeds

Combine ingredients. Cover; chill 2 hours to blend flavors. Makes about 3/4 cup.

Per tablespoon:

CAL	PRO	CARB	FIB	FAT	SAT	CHOL	SOD
21	<1g	4g	0g	<1g	<1g	1mg	13mg

STEAMED ARTICHOKE WITH DILL DIP

TOP OF STOVE

2 artichokes
1 lemon, quartered
1/3 cup reduced calorie mayonnaise
1/2 teaspoon dill weed

Place artichokes in basket of large steamer. Add lemon to water in pan. Cover; steam 30 to 45 minutes or until leaves are tender (if they can be removed easily they are usually done). Combine mayonnaise and dill weed. Serve as a dip with artichokes. Serve artichokes warm or cold. Makes 8 servings.

Per serving:

CAL	PRO	CARB	FIB	FAT	SAT	CHOL	SOD
49	1g	4g	2g	3g	1g	3mg	105mg

HONEY PEANUT BUTTER SPREAD

Makes a nutritious snack on apple and pear slices, crackers and peanut butter sandwiches.

1/3 cup creamy peanut butter
2 tablespoons honey

Combine ingredients; mix to blend. Store in covered container in refrigerator. If chilled, let soften at room temperature before serving. Makes 7 tablespoons.

Per tablespoon:

CAL	PRO	CARB	FIB	FAT	SAT	CHOL	SOD
90	3g	7g	1g	6g	1g	0mg	59mg

Cook's Tip

Red peppers make attractive serving bowls. Lay pepper on its side, cut a slice off the top and hollow out center (do not remove stem). Fill with your favorite dip.

CAROLYN'S CRISP ASPARAGUS TIPS

TOP OF STOVE
CHILL

Kathy isn't too fond of some vegetables, but her mother's chilled asparagus and dip is a winner with her.

16 fresh thin asparagus spears
1/3 cup reduced calorie mayonnaise
1 1/2 teaspoons reduced sodium soy sauce (or to taste)

Wash asparagus; snap off at breaking point. Place in steamer rack over hot water; cover and steam 3 to 5 minutes or until just crisp tender. Chill until ready to serve. Combine mayonnaise and soy sauce. Chill to blend flavors.

Per one spear and 1 teaspoon dip:

CAL	PRO	CARB	FIB	FAT	SAT	CHOL	SOD
22	<1g	1g	<1g	2g	<1g	2mg	54mg

CELERY BOATS

CHILL

1 small bunch celery
1 (8-ounce) container Light cream cheese product, softened
1 (8-ounce) can crushed pineapple, drained thoroughly
Paprika

Trim celery stalks; wash and dry thoroughly. Combine cream cheese and pineapple. Spoon mixture into celery stalks; level off top with a knife. Sprinkle very lightly with paprika. Place on tray and chill. When ready to serve, cut into 2-inch pieces. Place on attractive serving plate. Makes about 60 appetizers.

Per 2-inch piece:

CAL	PRO	CARB	FIB	FAT	SAT	CHOL	SOD
13	<1g	1g	<1g	<1g	1g	1mg	31mg

APPETIZER CUCUMBER ROUNDS

These can be made ahead, but to keep from drying out, they need to be covered with a damp towel and refrigerated.

1 (1 pound) loaf cocktail rye bread
1 (8-ounce) container Light cream cheese product, softened
1 medium cucumber
Fresh parsley

Spread each bread slice with 1 teaspoon cream cheese. Flute cucumber by running tines of fork down the sides. Cut into thin slices. Place two slices, overlapping on bread. Garnish with a small sprig of parsley. Makes 40 appetizers.

Per appetizer:

CAL	PRO	CARB	FIB	FAT	SAT	CHOL	SOD
41	2g	7g	<1g	1g	<1g	2mg	95mg

BASIL

NACHOS

OVEN 425°

Chicken mixture can be made ahead and reheated.

1 pound ground lean chicken
1 cup thick and chunky salsa (plus some for serving, if desired)
6 ounces round tortilla chips
1 cup (4-ounces) low fat Cheddar cheese, shredded
1 plum tomato, diced

In medium skillet, brown ground chicken, breaking it up into small pieces as it cooks. Drain off liquid. Add salsa. Simmer 8 to 10 minutes or until liquid is absorbed. Place tortilla chips in 12-inch pizza pan, filling in to completely cover pan. Spoon chicken over chips. Sprinkle with cheese. Bake at 425° until cheese is melted. Remove from oven; sprinkle tomatoes over top. Serves 6 as an appetizer.

TIP: If desired, serve topped with additional salsa and just a dab of light sour cream.

Per serving:

CAL	PRO	CARB	FIB	FAT	SAT	CHOL	SOD
312	8g	20g	2g	19g	na	63mg	350mg

QUESADILLAS

OVEN 400°

Crushed pineapple adds a nice touch to these popular appetizers. Also good served with a chunky salsa.

6 (8-inch) flour tortillas
2 plum tomatoes, finely chopped
2 green onions, sliced thin
2 tablespoons chopped chilies
1 (8-ounce) can crushed pineapple, drained thoroughly
1 cup (4-ounces) reduced fat Monterey Jack cheese, shredded

Top half of each tortilla with some of the tomato, onion, chilies and pineapple. Sprinkle with some of the cheese. Place on baking sheet. Bake at 400° for 3 minutes or until cheese is melted. Remove from oven. Carefully fold each tortilla in half. Press edges to seal. Gently pat quesadilla to evenly distribute filling. Cut each into 4 wedges. Serve hot. Makes 24 appetizers.

Per appetizer:

CAL	PRO	CARB	FIB	FAT	SAT	CHOL	SOD
49	2g	7g	<1g	2g	<1g	3mg	61mg

OYSTERS IN THE SHELL

BROIL

If you like oysters, you will enjoy these.

Per oyster:

1 oyster, in shell
1 tablespoon seafood cocktail sauce
1/4 strip of bacon, slightly cooked
1 teaspoon grated Parmesan cheese

Open oyster, leaving oyster in the deeper side of shell. Cover with cocktail sauce. Top with bacon. Sprinkle with Parmesan. Place under broiler; broil until cheese is lightly browned. Serve hot. Makes 1 appetizer.

Per (3/4-ounce meat portion) appetizer:

CAL	PRO	CARB	FIB	FAT	SAT	CHOL	SOD
66	6g	6g	<1g	2g	<1g	24mg	326mg

RAW VEGETABLE TRAY

A tray of attractively cut and arranged fresh vegetables will be healthy for you and make your diet conscious guests happy.

SUGGESTIONS:
Asparagus spears
Broccoli and cauliflower flowerettes
Carrot strips or curls
Celery sticks
Cherry tomatoes
Cucumber spears
Green onions
Red, yellow and green pepper strips
Mushrooms
Radishes
Snow peas
Zucchini rounds or spears

TIP: You could also serve a tray of assorted fruits or fruit kabobs.

NOTE: Nutritional Analysis is impossible to determine, but as you can see, you can eat to your "hearts" delight and not have to worry about the fat or cholesterol content.

Smoked Salmon Cucumber Canapés

These make an attractive canapé tray; they go fast, so make plenty.

For each canapé:

1 slice party rye bread
1 teaspoon Light cream cheese product, softened
2 thin slices cucumber
1 small thin slice smoked salmon, about 1 x 2 inches (3/4-ounce)
Sprigs of fresh dill or parsley

Spread each bread slice with cream cheese. Score cucumbers by running a sharp tined fork down length of cucumber. Cut into thin slices. Top bread with two cucumber slices slightly over-lapping. Arrange salmon on top. Garnish with small sprig of dill or parsley.

Per canapé:

Cal	Pro	Carb	Fib	Fat	Sat	Chol	Sod
66	6g	7g	<1g	2g	<1g	7mg	264mg

Sweet-Sour Meatball Appetizer

Top of Stove

If you haven't tried turkey sausage, you will have to try this recipe.

1 (16-ounce) package frozen turkey sausage, thawed
1 (10-ounce) jar apricot preserves
1 cup thick and rich barbecue sauce
1 (16-ounce) can pineapple chunks, drained
1 (8-ounce) can whole water chestnuts, drained, cut in half
1 large green pepper, cut into 1-inch chunks

Form sausage into 46 meatballs the size of large marbles. Place in nonstick skillet; cook until lightly browned and cooked through. Drain off fat. Meanwhile, combine remaining ingredients in medium saucepan. Bring to a boil; add meatballs. Reduce heat; simmer 8 to 10 minutes or until green pepper is crisp tender. Keep hot in chafing dish or on warming tray. Makes 23 servings of 2 meatballs each.

Per serving:

Cal	Pro	Carb	Fib	Fat	Sat	Chol	Sod
96	4g	14g	<1g	3g	1g	16mg	148mg

TERIYAKI CHICKEN WINGS

MARINATE
OVEN 350°

A richly glazed appetizer that can also be served as a main dish.

16 chicken drumettes (the meaty leg portion of wings)
1/4 cup reduced sodium soy sauce
3/4 cup firmly packed light brown sugar
1 tablespoon honey
4 thin slices fresh ginger
2 green onions, cut into 1-inch pieces

Clean wings; trim off excess fat and skin. Place in medium bowl. Combine remaining ingredients; stir to dissolve sugar. Pour over chicken. Cover; chill at least 3 hours, turning occasionally. When ready to bake, place chicken in foil lined shallow baking pan. Bake at 350° for 15 minutes. Baste with marinade; bake 30 to 35 minutes or until tender, basting frequently. (Remove skin before eating.) Makes 8 hors d'oeuvre servings of 2 each.

Per servings:

CAL	PRO	CARB	FIB	FAT	SAT	CHOL	SOD
117	10g	10g	0g	3g	<1g	27mg	149mg

TERIYAKI KABOBS

MARINATE
GRILL

These go fast. Skewers should be soaked in water for 20 minutes.

1 pound beef sirloin
1/3 cup brown sugar
1/3 cup reduced sodium soy sauce
2 tablespoons white vinegar
1 1/2 tablespoons Worcestershire sauce
2 thin slices fresh ginger

Cut sirloin crosswise into long thin slices. In mixing bowl, combine remaining ingredients. Add meat; cover and marinate in refrigerator at least 2 hours. When ready to cook, thread about 2 strips on each 4-inch wooden skewer. Place on heated grill; cook about 2 minutes. Brush with marinade; turn and cook 1 to 2 minutes or until cooked to desired doneness. Makes 20 kabobs.

Per kabob:

CAL	PRO	CARB	FIB	FAT	SAT	CHOL	SOD
44	6g	<1g	0g	1g	<1g	16mg	60mg

CRANBERRY-STRAWBERRY PUNCH

CHILL

Nice served as a dessert drink or doubled for a party punch.

3 cups Cran-Strawberry cocktail
1 cup orange juice
2 tablespoons fresh lemon juice
1 quart diet ginger ale, chilled

Combine first 3 ingredient; chill until ready to serve. Add ginger ale. Makes 8 cups.

Per 1 cup serving:

CAL	PRO	CARB	FIB	FAT	SAT	CHOL	SOD
112	<1g	28g	<1g	<1g	0g	0mg	14mg

RASPBERRY PUNCH

Enjoy variety by substituting different flavors.

2 quarts raspberry sherbet
3 quarts 7-Up, chilled

Spoon sherbet into large punch bowl. Add 7-Up to taste, stirring carefully until most of the sherbet has melted and punch is a nice pink color. Makes 36 (4-ounce) servings.

Per serving:

CAL	PRO	CARB	FIB	FAT	SAT	CHOL	SOD
93	<1g	22g	0g	<1	<1	3mg	29mg

WHITE GRAPE SPRITZER

When you wish to relax and you want something cold, treat yourself to a satisfying thirst quenching non-alcoholic drink.

Per drink:
3/4 cup white grape juice
3/4 cup diet 7-up

Combine ingredients; pour over ice. Serve immediately. Makes 1 serving.

Per serving:

CAL	PRO	CARB	FIB	FAT	SAT	CHOL	SOD
116	1g	29g	1g	<1g	0g	0mg	22mg

PASSION PUNCH

TOP OF STOVE
CHILL

A nice hot weather punch to remind you of the tropics.

3/4 cup sugar
1 cup grapefruit juice
1/2 cup fresh orange juice
2 tablespoons fresh lemon juice
1/3 cup bottled grenadine syrup
6 cups diet ginger ale, chilled

In medium saucepan, combine sugar with 1 cup water. Bring to a boil; reduce heat and simmer 3 to 4 minutes or until sugar is dissolved. Cool. Combine grapefruit, orange and lemon juice with grenadine syrup. Chill until ready to serve. Add ginger ale. Makes 8 1/2 cups.

Per 1/2 cup serving:

CAL	PRO	CARB	FIB	FAT	SAT	CHOL	SOD
115	<1g	29g	<1g	<1g	0g	0mg	22mg

ORANGE FROST

Serve as a fruit drink or a light dessert.

1/2 cup orange juice
1/2 cup nonfat milk
1 medium banana
1 pint orange sorbet

Combine ingredients in blender and blend on high speed until smooth. Blend until more liquid for a fruit drink, but leave thick for a dessert. Serve in your most attractive wine glasses. Makes 3 one cup servings.

Per serving:

CAL	PRO	CARB	FIB	FAT	SAT	CHOL	SOD
271	2g	38g	1g	<1g	<1g	<1mg	26mg

HOT APPLE CIDER

TOP OF STOVE

2 quarts apple cider
1/4 cup firmly packed light brown sugar
2 cinnamon sticks
1 1/2 teaspoons whole allspice
20 whole cloves
1 small orange, cut into 1/4-inch slices, do not peel

Place all ingredients in a large pot. Bring to a simmer and heat 10 to 12 minutes to blend flavors. Serve hot. Makes 8 one cup servings.

Per serving:

CAL	PRO	CARB	FIB	FAT	SAT	CHOL	SOD
142	<1g	36g	<1g	<1g	0g	0mg	10mg

SPICED COFFEE

TOP OF STOVE

4 cups water
1 cinnamon stick
1 teaspoon whole allspice
Dash nutmeg
2 small packages artificial sweetener
1 tablespoon instant regular or decaffeinated coffee

In large saucepan, combine first 4 ingredients. Bring mixture to a boil; remove from heat. Stir in sweetener and coffee. Serve hot. Makes 4 servings.

Per serving:

CAL	PRO	CARB	FIB	FAT	SAT	CHOL	SOD
4	<1g	<1g	<1g	<1g	<1g	0mg	20mg

Breads

WHOLE WHEAT BREAD

OVEN 375°

Enjoy the delightful aroma of bread fresh from the oven.

1 package dry yeast
2 tablespoons honey
2 tablespoons stick margarine (cut into small pieces)
1 teaspoon salt
1$^{1}/_{2}$ cups all-purpose flour
1$^{1}/_{2}$ cups whole wheat flour, divided

Add yeast and honey to 1$^{1}/_{4}$ cups warm water (105° to 115°). Let stand 10 minutes. In large mixer bowl, combine yeast mixture with margarine, salt, all-purpose flour and $^{1}/_{2}$ cup of the whole wheat flour. On low speed, beat until blended. Beat at medium speed for 1 minute. Stir in remaining 1 cup whole wheat flour by hand. Cover; let rise in warm place until doubled in size, about 60 minutes. Stir down; spoon into 9 x 5-inch loaf pan sprayed with vegetable cooking spray. Let rise until doubled in size about 45 minutes. Bake at 375° for 35 to 45 minutes or until tests done. Remove from pan; cool on rack. Makes 1 loaf of 16 slices.

VARIATION: For white bread, use all white flour.

Per slice:

CAL	PRO	CARB	FIB	FAT	SAT	CHOL	SOD
103	3g	20g	2g	2g	<1g	0mg	151mg

JALAPEÑO CORN BREAD

OVEN 425°

A moist corn bread.

2 (8$^{3}/_{4}$-ounce) packages corn bread mix
2 eggs
1 (4-ounce) can green chiles
1 (8$^{3}/_{4}$-ounce) can creamed corn
3 tablespoons finely chopped onion
1 cup (4-ounces) reduced fat Cheddar cheese, shredded

In large mixing bowl, combine all the ingredients along with 1 cup water. Stir just enough to moisten. Pour into 8 x 8-inch baking dish sprayed with vegetable cooking spray. Bake at 425° for 35 to 40 minutes or until lightly browned. Makes 9 servings.

Per serving:

CAL	PRO	CARB	FIB	FAT	SAT	CHOL	SOD
311	9g	47g	<1g	10g	2g	56mg	606mg

FOCACCIA

OVEN 425°

Sit back and enjoy the compliments when you serve this bread. Also makes a delicious sandwich bread.

1 package dry yeast
2 to 2 1/2 cups flour, divided
1 teaspoon sugar
1/2 teaspoon salt
1 tablespoon, plus 1 teaspoon olive oil, divided
Garlic salt or grated Parmesan cheese

In large mixer bowl, combine yeast, 1 1/2 cups of the flour, sugar and salt. Add 3/4 cup hot tap water and the 1 tablespoon olive oil. Beat until smooth. By hand, stir in enough of the remaining flour to make a soft, but not sticky dough. On lightly floured surface, knead about 5 minutes. Place in lightly greased bowl. Cover and set in warm place until doubled, about 60 minutes. Lightly spray 12-inch pizza pan or large baking sheet with vegetable cooking spray. With fingers, flatten dough into an 11-inch circle. Prick surface of dough with a fork. Brush with 1 teaspoon olive oil. Sprinkle lightly with garlic salt or Parmesan cheese. Let rise in warm place 30 minutes. Bake at 425° 18 to 20 minutes or until golden. Best served warm. Makes 10 servings.

VARIATION: Brush with oil. Top with 2/3 cup narrow strips red and green peppers. Sprinkle with 1/4 cup (1-ounce) Lite Mozzarella cheese, shredded.

Per serving:

CAL	PRO	CARB	FIB	FAT	SAT	CHOL	SOD
122	3g	22g	1g	2g	<1g	0mg	150mg

QUICK FOCACCIA

OVEN 350°

A nice crisp bread to serve with soups or salads.

1 can refrigerated bread sticks
1 teaspoon olive oil
1/2 teaspoon basil
1/2 teaspoon rosemary
1/2 teaspoon garlic powder

Separate bread sticks, but do not unroll. Place on baking sheet sprayed with vegetable cooking spray. Press into 4-inch circles. Brush lightly with olive oil. Combine remaining ingredients; sprinkle over dough. Bake at 350° for 12 to 15 minutes or until lightly browned. Makes 8 servings.

Per serving:

CAL	PRO	CARB	FIB	FAT	SAT	CHOL	SOD
71	2g	<1g	<1g	2g	<1g	0mg	113mg

PIZZA DOUGH

An easy to make next-to-no-fat pizza dough.

1 package dry yeast
1 1/2 cups water, divided
3 1/4 to 4 cups flour
1/2 teaspoon salt

Dissolve yeast in 1/2 cup warm water (105° to 115°). Let stand 5 to 10 minutes. In large mixing bowl, combine yeast mixture and remaining 1 cup water. Combine 3 1/4 cups flour with salt; add to yeast mixture. Stir to form a fairly stiff dough that is barely sticky and can be kneaded, adding more flour if necessary. Place on lightly floured surface; knead 5 to 10 minutes or until elastic to the touch. Place in large bowl sprayed with vegetable cooking spray. Lightly spray top of dough. Cover; let rise about 60 minutes or until doubled. Press dough into pans, add toppings and bake.

TIP: For thin crisp crust, the dough will make two 16-inch pizzas. For a thicker crust you can make two 12-inch pizzas. Or it will make five 9-inch crusts for individual pie tin pizzas.

Per recipe:

CAL	PRO	CARB	FIB	FAT	SAT	CHOL	SOD
1612	48g	337g	14g	4g	<1g	0mg	1089mg

ITALIAN BREAD PIZZA SHELL

OVEN 400°

Purchased bread shells are very expensive. Now you can make your own.

1 loaf frozen white bread dough, thawed
1/4 cup (1-ounce) Lite Mozzarella cheese, shredded
1 tablespoon grated Parmesan cheese

Shape dough into a ball. Let rest 10 minutes. Roll on lightly floured surface into a 14-inch round. At first, the dough is quite difficult to roll. If it continues to be difficult to roll, let stand another 5 minutes. Place round on 12-inch pizza pan sprayed lightly with vegetable cooking spray. Fold edges over toward inside of pan making a thick rim. Press to seal. Sprinkle with cheeses. Bake at 400° for 13 to 15 minutes or until just lightly browned. Remove from pan; cool on rack. Bread is ready to use or can be tightly wrapped and frozen. Makes 8 servings.

TIP: Use assorted toppings for pizzas or snacks.

Per serving:

CAL	PRO	CARB	FIB	FAT	SAT	CHOL	SOD
168	7g	31g	1g	1g	<1g	1mg	

BANANA BREAD

OVEN 350°

Everyone's favorite. A delicious way to use up those too ripe bananas.

1/2 cup soft tub margarine
1 cup sugar
1/2 cup egg substitute
1 cup mashed very ripe bananas
1 1/4 cups flour
1 teaspoon baking soda

In mixer bowl, cream margarine and sugar, slowly add egg substitute. Beat until smooth and and no longer looks curdled. Add bananas. Combine flour and baking soda. Add to banana mixture; stir just enough to moisten flour. Pour into two 7 x 5-inch loaf pans sprayed with vegetable cooking spray. Bake at 350° for 30 to 40 minutes or until tests done. Remove from pans; let cool on rack. Makes 2 loaves of 10 slices each.

Per slice:

CAL	PRO	CARB	FIB	FAT	SAT	CHOL	SOD
120	1g	19g	<1g	5g	<1g	0mg	87mg

STRAWBERRY FUN BREAD

OVEN 350°

I call this fun bread because of the color and the fun you can have serving it to your friends. It is red, pink and purple. Give this bread a try, the flavor is wonderful.

1/2 cup egg substitute
1/2 cup Canola oil
1 (10-ounce) package frozen sliced strawberries with juice, thawed
1 cup sugar
1 3/4 cups flour
1 teaspoon baking soda

In mixer bowl, beat egg substitute and oil until blended. Add strawberries; beat until well mixed and berries are broken up. Combine remaining ingredients. Add to berry mixture, stirring just enough to moisten flour. Pour into two 7x3-inch loaf pans sprayed with vegetable cooking spray. Bake at 350° for 35 to 45 minutes or until tests done. Remove from oven; let stand 5 minutes. Remove from pans; cool on rack. Makes 20 serving (10 slices per loaf).

Per slice:

CAL	PRO	CARB	FIB	FAT	SAT	CHOL	SOD
143	2g	22g	<1g	6g	<1g	0mg	50mg

DATE NUT BREAD

TOP OF STOVE
OVEN 350°

Allow time for the dates to cool.

2 cups coarsely cut-up dates
1/2 cup stick margarine, softened
2 cups sugar
4 cups flour
1 tablespoon baking soda
3/4 cup coarsely chopped pecans

Add dates to 2 cups boiling water. Let stand to cool (this will probably take an hour or so). In large mixer bowl, beat margarine and sugar until blended. Combine flour and baking soda; add to sugar mixture, mix well. Stir in pecans. Add 1 cup of date mixture; mix until blended. Add remaining date mixture. Pour into 2 greased 9 x 5-inch loaf pans sprayed with vegetable cooking spray. Bake at 350° for 55 to 60 minutes or until tests done. Remove from oven; let stand 5 minutes. Remove from pans; cool on rack. Makes two loaves, 16 slices per loaf.

Per slice:

CAL	PRO	CARB	FIB	FAT	SAT	CHOL	SOD
177	2g	33g	2g	5g	<1g	0mg	102mg

QUICK BROWN BREAD

OVEN 350°

This is a delicious moist quick bread similar to bran muffins.

3/4 cup flour
2 cups whole wheat flour
1 cup firmly packed light brown sugar
2 teaspoons baking soda
1/2 teaspoon salt
2 cups buttermilk

Place first five ingredients in medium bowl. Stir to mix making sure there are no sugar lumps. Gradually stir in buttermilk. Pour into 9 x 5 -inch loaf pan sprayed with vegetable cooking spray. Bake at 350° for 45 to 55 minutes or until browned and cooked through. Makes 1 large loaf of 16 servings.

TIP: Bread may appear to be done when it isn't. Check carefully.

Per slice:

CAL	PRO	CARB	FIB	FAT	SAT	CHOL	SOD
136	4g	30g	2g	<1g	<1g	1mg	206

QUICK METHOD GRAHAM BREAD

OVEN 375°

A moist slightly heavy bread best served warm. Makes good sandwich bread.

2 cups graham flour (or whole wheat)
1 cup flour
1/2 cup sugar
1 teaspoon salt
1 teaspoon baking soda
2 cups buttermilk

Combine both flours, sugar and salt. Combine baking soda and buttermilk. Stir into flour mixture just until blended. Pour into 9 x 5-inch loaf pan sprayed lightly with vegetable cooking spray. Bake at 375° for 60 to 70 minutes or until tests done. Remove from pans and cool on rack. Makes 1 loaf of 16 slices.

Per slice:

CAL	PRO	CARB	FIB	FAT	SAT	CHOL	SOD
116	4g	25g	2g	<1g	<1g	1mg	218mg

SCONES

OVEN 450°

These can be quickly made for breakfast, lunch, dinner or a snack - actually good any time. Serve with a delicious jam and omit the butter.

2 cups self-rising flour
2 tablespoons sugar, plus 1 teaspoon, divided
1/4 cup soft tub margarine (as cold as possible)
1/2 cup raisins
1/4 cup egg substitute
2/3 cup, plus 2 tablespoons buttermilk

In large mixing bowl, combine flour and the two tablespoons sugar. Drop margarine in small pieces over flour. Mix with a fork until mixture resembles coarse crumbs. Stir in raisins. Combine egg substitute and buttermilk. Add to flour mixture; stir until flour is moistened. Turn out onto well-floured surface (mixture will be quite sticky). Gently knead until smooth. Form into a ball; place on baking sheet sprayed with vegetable cooking spray. Pat dough into about an 8-inch circle, 1/2-inch thick. Carefully cut in half crosswise. Cut each half into 4 wedges, cutting all the way through, but do not separate. Sprinkle with the 1 teaspoon sugar. Bake at 450° for 10 to 12 minutes or until golden. Serve hot. Makes 8 servings.

Per scone:

CAL	PRO	CARB	FIB	FAT	SAT	CHOL	SOD
215	5g	35g	1g	6g	1g	<1mg	481mg

THE BASIC MUFFIN

OVEN 400°

Nothing fancy, but good with almost any meal.

2 cups flour
1/2 cup sugar
1 tablespoon baking powder
5 tablespoons vegetable oil
2 egg whites
3/4 cup nonfat milk

Combine first 3 ingredients in medium bowl, stirring to blend. Combine remaining ingredients in a small bowl; pour into flour mixture. Stir gently just until flour is moistened. Spoon into paper-lined muffin tins, filling about 2/3 full. Bake at 400° for 18 to 20 minutes or until light golden and tests done. Makes 12 muffins.

VARIATIONS: Add one or two of the following, if desired

1 cup blueberries
1/2 cup chopped nuts
1 tablespoon freshly grated lemon peel
1 tablespoon freshly grated orange peel
1 teaspoon jam
Dip tops in melted soft tub margarine and then in cinnamon sugar

Per muffin:

CAL	PRO	CARB	FIB	FAT	SAT	CHOL	SOD
167	3g	25g	<1g	6g	<1g	<1mg	100mg

BANANA MUFFINS

OVEN 375°

A tasty way to use up those too ripe bananas.

1/2 cup sugar
1 cup self-rising flour
1/2 teaspoon baking soda
1 cup mashed bananas
2 egg whites
1/4 cup Canola oil

In mixing bowl, combine sugar, flour and baking soda. Combine remaining ingredients with 1 tablespoon water; stir into flour mixture just until moistened. Spoon into muffin tins sprayed with vegetable cooking spray filling 2/3 full. Bake at 375° for 10 to 12 minutes or until done. Makes 12 muffins.

Per muffin:

CAL	PRO	CARB	FIB	FAT	SAT	CHOL	SOD
129	2g	21g	<1g	5g	<1g	0mg	176mg

FEATHER LIGHT MUFFINS

OVEN 400°

A light not too sweet muffin. Best served hot from the oven.

1/2 cup soft tub margarine
1/3 cup sugar
2 egg whites
1 tablespoon baking powder
1 1/2 cups flour
3/4 cup nonfat milk

In large mixer bowl, cream margarine and sugar. Add egg white; beat until blended. Combine baking powder and flour, Add flour mixture to creamed mixture, alternately with the milk, starting and ending with flour. Spoon into muffin tins sprayed with vegetable cooking spray, filling 3/4 full. Bake at 400° for 18 to 20 minutes or until tests done. Makes 12 muffins.

TIP: If desired, sprinkle a little sugar over batter before baking.

Per muffin:

CAL	PRO	CARB	FIB	FAT	SAT	CHOL	SOD
154	3g	19g	<1g	8g	1g	<1mg	163mg

LEMON MUFFINS

OVEN 400°

You will enjoy these tart, not too sweet muffins. Delicious served with marmalade.

2 cups flour
2/3 cup sugar, plus 2 teaspoons, divided
1 tablespoon baking powder
1/2 cup soft tub margarine, melted
1/2 cup egg substitute
2 lemons (you will need 1/2 cup juice and 1 tablespoon grated peel)

In medium mixing bowl, combine flour, 2/3 cup sugar and baking powder. Combine melted margarine, egg substitute, lemon juice and peel. Pour over flour mixture. Stir, just enough to moisten. Spoon into muffin tins sprayed with vegetable cooking spray. Sprinkle each muffin lightly with remaining sugar. Bake at 400° for 15 to 18 minutes or until tests done. Makes 12 muffins.

Per muffin:

CAL	PRO	CARB	FIB	FAT	SAT	CHOL	SOD
195	3g	29g	<1g	8g	1g	0mg	159mg

ORANGE MINI MUFFINS

OVEN 425°

A delightful orange flavored muffin.

2 large oranges
2 cups flour
1/2 cup sugar
1 tablespoon baking powder
5 tablespoons soft tub margarine
2 egg whites

Grate oranges to measure 2 teaspoons orange peel. Squeeze to make 1/2 cup juice. In medium mixing bowl, combine flour, sugar and baking powder. Cut in margarine. Combine orange peel, juice and egg whites. Add to flour mixture; stir just enough to moisten. Spray mini muffin tins lightly with vegetable cooking spray. Fill 2/3 full. Bake at 425° for 8 to 10 minutes or until golden. Makes 36 muffins.

TIP: If larger muffins are desired, completely fill muffin tin. You will have a very attractive muffin with a larger dome.

Per mini muffin:

CAL	PRO	CARB	FIB	FAT	SAT	CHOL	SOD
53	1g	9g	<1g	2g	<1g	0mg	44mg

Whole Wheat Muffins

Oven 375°

Serve hot and fresh from the oven.

2 cups whole wheat flour
1/2 cup sugar
3 1/2 teaspoons baking powder
2 egg whites
3 tablespoons soft tub margarine
1 1/2 cups nonfat milk

In mixing bowl, combine flour, sugar and baking powder. Combine remaining ingredients. Add to dry mixture; stir just enough to moisten (do not overmix). Pour into muffin tins sprayed with vegetable cooking spray, filling 3/4 full. Bake at 375° for 25 to 30 minutes or until tests done. Makes 12 muffins.

Per muffin:

Cal	Pro	Carb	Fib	Fat	Sat	Chol	Sod
139	4g	25g	3g	3g	<1g	0mg	145mg

Quick Cinnamon Rolls

Oven 375°

These can be ready to go in the oven in less then 5 minutes.

1 (10-ounce) can refrigerated pizza crust
1 tablespoon soft tub margarine
2 tablespoons cinnamon sugar
1/2 cup sifted powdered sugar
2 teaspoons light corn syrup

Spray 8-inch cake pan with vegetable cooking spray. Unroll pizza dough; press slightly to straighten edges. You should have about a 10 x 13-inch rectangle. Spread margarine evenly over dough. Sprinkle with cinnamon sugar. Roll up tightly, starting with 10-inch side. Press edges to seal. Cut into 8 slices. Place, cut side up, in cake pan. Bake at 375° for 18 to 20 minutes or until golden. Remove from pan; place right side up on serving dish. Combine powdered sugar and corn syrup with just enough water to make a glaze, blending until smooth. Drizzle over hot rolls; serve hot. Makes 8 rolls.

Per roll:

Cal	Pro	Carb	Fib	Fat	Sat	Chol	Sod
142	3g	26g	<1g	2g	<1g	0mg	183mg

BISCUITS

OVEN 450°

Buttermilk biscuits are always a favorite, but these are just as good with even less fat.

2 cups flour
1/2 teaspoon salt
3 teaspoons baking powder
1 tablespoon, plus 2 teaspoons melted, soft tub margarine
3/4 cup nonfat milk

In medium mixing bowl, combine flour, salt and baking powder. Stir to mix. Add the 1 tablespoon margarine to the milk. Add to flour mixture; stir quickly and gently to blend. Place on lightly floured surface. Knead lightly until smooth (this doesn't take long). Gently pat into a round about 3/4-inch thick. Cut with 2 1/2-inch biscuit cutter into 12 biscuits. Scraps can be gently re-rolled. Place on baking sheet sprayed with vegetable cooking spray. Brush lightly with remaining margarine. Bake at 450° for 10 to 12 minutes or until light golden. Makes 12 biscuits.

TIP: For crisp biscuits, do not allow biscuits to touch. For softer biscuits, place biscuits close together on baking sheet or in 8 x 8-inch baking pan.

Per biscuit:

CAL	PRO	CARB	FIB	FAT	SAT	CHOL	SOD
95	3g	17g	<1g	2g	<1g	0mg	316mg

Cook's Tip

ALWAYS, ALWAYS, ALWAYS
read through a new recipe before you begin.

BUTTERMILK BISCUITS

OVEN 400°

The margarine in the recipe makes a nice golden biscuit.

2 cups flour
2 teaspoons baking powder
3/4 teaspoon baking soda
1 tablespoon sugar
5 tablespoons soft tub margarine
1 cup buttermilk

In medium bowl, combine flour, baking powder, baking soda and sugar. Add margarine; cut in with a fork or pastry blender until very small balls form. Add buttermilk; stir just until moistened. Mixture will be quite moist. Turn out on floured surface. Gently knead, about 10 to 15 turns, until smooth. Dough will be quite soft and feel light to the touch. Pat out 1/2 -inch thick. Cut with floured 2-inch round cutter (do not twist, but cut straight down). Place on baking sheet sprayed with vegetable cooking spray. Bake at 400° for 10 to 12 minutes or until cooked through and golden. Makes 20 2-inch biscuits.

TIP: Scraps can be used, but treat gently or biscuits will be tough.

Per biscuit:

CAL	PRO	CARB	FIB	FAT	SAT	CHOL	SOD
78	2g	11g	<1g	3g	<1g	<1mg	100mg

Cakes
Cookies
Desserts
& Pies

ANGEL FOOD CAKE

OVEN 350°

A melt in your mouth, made from scratch cake. Try a variety of fruit toppings for a delicious no-fat dessert.

1½ cups egg whites (11 to 12 large eggs)
1½ teaspoons cream of tartar
1 teaspoon vanilla extract (use clear vanilla if you have it)
1 cup sugar
1½ cups sifted powdered sugar
1 cup cake flour

In large mixing bowl, combine egg whites, cream of tartar and vanilla. Beat until soft peaks form. Gradually add the granulated sugar, about 2 tablespoons at a time. Beat until stiff peaks form. Combine powdered sugar and cake flour; blend thoroughly. Add flour mixture, about ⅓ cup at a time, to beaten egg whites, folding in lightly by hand. Spoon into ungreased 10-inch Angel Food cake pan. Bake on lowest rack in 350° oven for 40 to 45 minutes or until tests done. Invert cake pan (on neck of narrow bottle); cool. Remove from pan. Makes 16 servings.

Per serving:

CAL	PRO	CARB	FIB	FAT	SAT	CHOL	SOD
121	3g	27g	<1g	0g	0g	0mg	38mg

APRICOT CAKE

OVEN 350°

A favorite in my family. Do not use substitutes for the eggs in this recipe.

¾ cup sugar, plus 1 tablespoon
2 eggs
5 tablespoons soft tub margarine, melted
¾ cup flour
1 (16-ounce) can apricot halves, drained

In mixer bowl, combine the ¾ cup sugar and eggs. Beat at high speed until smooth. Add melted margarine and flour; mix well. Pour into 8 x 8-inch baking pan sprayed with vegetable cooking spray. Sprinkle with remaining 1 tablespoon sugar. Arrange apricot halves, rounded-side up, on batter. Bake at 350° (325° if using glass) for 35 to 40 minutes or until cake tests done. Serve warm or cold. Makes 9 servings.

Per serving:

CAL	PRO	CARB	FIB	FAT	SAT	CHOL	SOD
201	3g	32g	1g	7g	1g	47mg	69mg

ORANGE CAKE

OVEN 350°

Simple, yet festive.

1 (18¼-ounce) package white Mrs. Wright's Deluxe 3 in 1 Cake Mix (Lite recipe uses no oil)
1⅓ cups orange juice
2 egg whites
1 (8-ounce) container Lite frozen whipped topping, thawed
1 (16-ounce) can light cherry pie filling

In large mixing bowl, combine dry mix, orange juice and egg whites. Beat on low until blended. Beat on medium speed 2 to 3 minutes or until smooth. Pour into 9 x 13-inch baking dish sprayed with vegetable cooking spray. Bake at 350° (325° if using glass) for 25 to 30 minutes or until cake tests done. Let cool. Cut into 15 squares. Serve each square with 2 tablespoons pie filling topped with 2 tablespoons whipped topping. Makes 15 servings.

Per serving:

CAL	PRO	CARB	FIB	FAT	SAT	CHOL	SOD
211	2	40g	<1g	7g	na	na	230mg

QUICK STIR CHOCOLATE CAKE

OVEN 375°

A very moist dark chocolate cake. For an added treat, top with vanilla ice milk or sprinkle lightly with powdered sugar.

1 cup sugar
⅓ cup cocoa
1½ cups flour
1 teaspoon baking soda
½ cup Canola oil
2 tablespoons white vinegar

Combine first 4 ingredients in large mixing bowl. Add oil and 1 cup cold water, stir with a fork to blend thoroughly. Quickly stir in vinegar. Pour into 8 x 8-inch baking dish sprayed with vegetable cooking spray. Gently drop on counter to eliminate bubbles. Bake at 375° (350° if using glass) for 25 to 30 minutes or until cake tests done. Makes 9 servings.

Per serving:

CAL	PRO	CARB	FIB	FAT	SAT	CHOL	SOD
312	3g	45g	2g	15g	1g	0mg	129mg

STRAWBERRY BOX CAKE

OVEN 350°
CHILL

If in season, top each serving with a beautiful red strawberry.

1 (18 1/4-ounce) package white Mrs. Wright's Deluxe 3 in 1 Cake Mix (Lite recipe - uses no oil)
1 1/3 cups water
2 egg whites
1 (3-ounce) package strawberry jello
1 cup boiling water
1 (8-ounce) container Lite frozen whipped topping, thawed

In large mixer bowl, combine cake mix, water and egg whites. Mix on low speed until moistened. Mix on high speed until well blended, about 2 minutes. Pour into 9 x 13-inch baking pan sprayed with vegetable cooking spray. Bake at 350° for 30 to 35 minutes or until tests done. Remove from oven; pierce cake all over with long-tined fork. Dissolve jello in boiling water; pour evenly over cake. Cover and chill. Spread whipped topping over top. Cover; chill until ready to serve. Makes 15 servings.

Per serving:

CAL	PRO	CARB	FIB	FAT	SAT	CHOL	SOD
197	4g	34g	0g	7g	na	na	234mg

COFFEE CAKE

OVEN 375°

This is a plain type coffee cake best served warm with jam or a topping of fresh fruit. Also good with light cherry pie filling.

3/4 cup sugar
1/4 cup soft tub margarine
1/4 cup egg substitute
1/2 cup nonfat milk
1 1/2 cups flour
2 teaspoons baking powder

In mixer bowl, mix thoroughly the sugar, margarine and egg substitute. Add milk; mix until smooth. Combine flour and baking powder. Add to creamed mixture, beating until blended. Pour into 8 x 8-inch baking dish sprayed with vegetable cooking spray. Bake at 375° (350° if using glass) for 25 to 30 minutes or until cake tests done. Makes 9 servings.

Per serving:

CAL	PRO	CARB	FIB	FAT	SAT	CHOL	SOD
193	3g	34g	<1g	5g	<1g	<1mg	132mg

BLUEBERRY COFFEECAKE

OVEN 375°

Watch the fat grams in this recipe and plan accordingly. Nice for brunch, holidays and special occasions.

3/4 cup soft tub margarine, divided
1 1/3 cups sugar, divided
4 egg whites
1 3/4 cups flour, divided
1 teaspoon baking powder
1 cup fresh or frozen blueberries (do not thaw)

In mixer bowl, cream 1/2 cup of the margarine and 1 cup of the sugar. Add egg whites, one at a time, mixing to blend. Combine 1 cup of the flour with the baking powder. Stir into creamed mixture. Gently fold in blueberries. Pour into 8 x 8-inch baking pan sprayed with vegetable cooking spray. Prepare Topping:

Combine remaining 1/3 cup sugar and 3/4 cup flour in small bowl. Add remaining 1/4 cup margarine; cut in with fork or pastry blender until mixture resembles tiny peas. Spoon evenly over batter. Bake at 375° (350° if using glass) for 40 to 50 minutes or until cake tests done. Makes 9 servings.

VARIATION: Omit blueberries. Using 1/4 cup raspberry preserves, drop small amounts over top of batter. Cut through batter with knife to marblize. Sprinkle with topping.

Per serving:

CAL	PRO	CARB	FIB	FAT	SAT	CHOL	SOD
353	4g	51g	1g	15g	3g	0mg	189mg

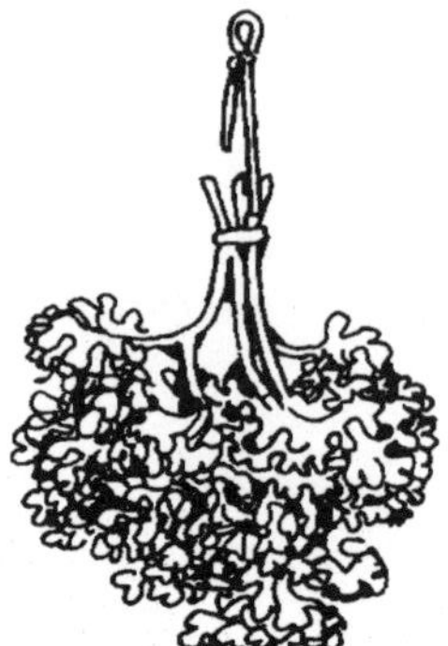

CRISP OATMEAL COOKIES

OVEN 350°

1 cup (2 sticks) margarine, softened slightly
1½ cups sugar
½ cup egg substitute
2 cups flour
1 teaspoon baking soda
3 cups old fashioned oats

Cream margarine and sugar in mixer bowl. Add egg substitute and mix until blended. Combine flour and baking soda; add to egg mixture. Add oatmeal; mix to blend. Drop by teaspoon onto baking sheets sprayed with vegetable cooking spray. Mounds should be slightly smaller than walnut size. Bake at 350° for 10 to 12 minutes or until golden. Makes 70 cookies.

Per cookie:

CAL	PRO	CARB	FIB	FAT	SAT	CHOL	SOD
66	1g	9g	<1g	3g	<1g	0mg	36mg

ORANGE CRISPIES

OVEN 375°

Very good served with a cup of coffee or a dish of frozen yogurt. Also good for lunch boxes.

1 cup sugar
1 cup soft tub margarine
1½ cups flour
2 egg whites
½ teaspoon orange extract
1 teaspoon freshly grated orange peel

In large mixer bowl, cream the sugar and margarine. Add remaining ingredients; beat until thoroughly blended. Drop by teaspoon onto ungreased cookie sheet, allowing at least 2½-inches between cookies (batter will spread). Bake at 375° for 8 to 10 minutes, or until just firm to the touch. Cookies may get quite brown around the edges, but remain white in the center. Let stand on cookie sheet about 1 minute before removing. Makes 40 cookies.

Per cookie:

CAL	PRO	CARB	FIB	FAT	SAT	CHOL	SOD
77	<1g	9g	<1g	4g	<1g	0mg	41mg

PEANUT BUTTER COOKIES

CHILL
OVEN 375°

Wonderful with a cup of coffee or hot tea. A favorite kids treat.

2 cups sugar
1 cup soft tub margarine
1 cup crunchy peanut butter
3 egg whites
3 cups flour
1½ teaspoons baking soda

In large mixer bowl, cream sugar, margarine and peanut butter. Add egg whites and mix well. Combine flour and baking soda. Add to creamed mixture. Cover and chill about 2 hours. Form into balls slightly smaller than a walnut. Place on ungreased cookie sheets and bake at 375° for 8 to 10 minutes. Makes 8 dozen cookies.

Per cookie:

CAL	PRO	CARB	FIB	FAT	SAT	CHOL	SOD
63	1g	8g	<1g	3g	<1g	0mg	43mg

RASPBERRY BARS

OVEN 350°

A nice addition to a cookie tray.

¾ cup quick-cooking oats
½ cup sugar
1 cup flour
½ cup stick margarine (chilled)
¼ cup sliced almonds
½ cup raspberry jam, plus 2 tablespoons

Place oats, sugar and flour in small mixing bowl. Cut margarine into small pieces; add to flour mixture. Cut in with 2 knives or a pastry blender to resemble coarse crumbs. Remove 1 cup mixture and combine with the almonds. Set aside. Press remaining crumb mixture evenly into 8 x 8-inch dish sprayed with vegetable cooking spray. Spread jam carefully over top spreading not quite to the edge. Sprinkle reserved almond mixture evenly over jam. Press gently. Bake at 350° for 25 to 30 minutes or until golden. Let cool on rack. Cut into bars. Makes 24.

Per cookie:

CAL	PRO	CARB	FIB	FAT	SAT	CHOL	SOD
107	1g	16g	<1g	5g	<1g	0mg	46mg

PEANUT BUTTER SNACK BARS

CHILL

Different, but good.

4 cups Rice Chex cereal
2 cups miniature pretzels, broken in half
3/4 cup raisins
5 tablespoons soft tub margarine
5 tablespoons chunky peanut butter
1 (10-ounce) package miniature marshmallows

In large mixing bowl, combine cereal, pretzels and raisins. In medium heavy saucepan, melt margarine, peanut butter and marshmallows over low heat, stirring occasionally until smooth. Pour over cereal mixture. Toss quickly to coat. Spoon into 9 x 13-inch baking pan sprayed with vegetable cooking spray. Press evenly into pan. Chill. Cut into 24 bars.

Per bar:

CAL	PRO	CARB	FIB	FAT	SAT	CHOL	SOD
124	2g	21g	<1g	4g	<1g	<1mg	143mg

CRISPY PIZZA TREAT

TOP OF STOVE

Kids love pizza in any form and they will enjoy this quick and easy treat. Don't expect any leftovers.

5 tablespoons soft tub margarine
1 (10-ounce) package large marshmallows
6 cups crispy rice cereal
1/2 of a 1-ounce square semi-sweet chocolate, melted

Melt margarine in large heavy saucepan over low heat. Add marshmallows; cook until melted, stirring frequently to blend. Stir in cereal to coat. Press evenly into 12-inch pizza pan sprayed with vegetable cooking spray. You need to work quickly. This is easier to do if you lightly butter your hands and use your fingers to press mixture into pan. Drizzle chocolate over top. Cool. Cut into 16 wedges.

Per wedge:

CAL	PRO	CARB	FIB	FAT	SAT	CHOL	SOD
135	1g	24g	<1g	4g	<1g	<1mg	167mg

KIX BARS

TOP OF STOVE

A good low-fat kid's snack.

7 cups Kix cereal
1 cup sugar
1/2 cup light corn syrup
1 tablespoon soft tub margarine
1 teaspoon vanilla extract

Place cereal in large mixing bowl. In medium saucepan, combine sugar, corn syrup, and margarine. Cook over medium heat until sugar dissolves, stirring frequently. Stir in vanilla. Pour over cereal; stir to coat. Spread in 11 x 7-inch dish sprayed with vegetable cooking spray. Press evenly in pan. Cool. Makes 24 bars.

Per bar:

CAL	PRO	CARB	FIB	FAT	SAT	CHOL	SOD
78	<1g	18g	0g	<1g	<1g	0mg	65mg

PECAN CRISPS

OVEN 375°

1 cup (2 sticks) margarine, softened slightly
1 cup sugar, plus 2 tablespoons
2 tablespoons nonfat milk
1 teaspoon vanilla extract
3 cups flour
3/4 cup chopped pecans

Cream margarine and the one cup sugar. Add milk and vanilla; mix well. Add flour; beat until blended. Stir in pecans. Drop by teaspoon onto baking sheets sprayed with vegetable cooking spray. Mounds should be slightly smaller than a walnut. Spread a small amount of margarine on the bottom of a flat bottomed drinking glass. Dip in remaining sugar. Press each cookie to about 1/4-inch thick; dipping in sugar each time. Bake at 375° for 10 to 12 minutes or until light golden around the edges. Makes 70 cookies.

Per cookie:

CAL	PRO	CARB	FIB	FAT	SAT	CHOL	SOD
63	<1g	8g	<1g	3g	<1g	0mg	22mg

OATMEAL SAUCEPAN COOKIES

TOP OF STOVE

2 cups sugar
6 tablespoons cocoa
1/2 cup soft tub margarine
1/2 cup nonfat milk
3 1/4 cups quick cooking oats

In medium saucepan, combine sugar and cocoa. Stir until well blended. Add margarine and milk. Bring to a boil, stirring occasionally. Remove from heat; stir in oatmeal to coat. Drop by teaspoons onto wax paper lined cookie sheet. Place in refrigerator until firm. Makes 45 cookies.

Per cookie:

CAL	PRO	CARB	FIB	FAT	SAT	CHOL	SOD
77	1g	13g	<1g	2g	<1g	0mg	24mg

Cook's Tip

In this book, soft tub margarine should be used straight from the refrigerator unless the recipe calls for melting.

ANGEL CAKE DESSERT

TOP OF STOVE

Keep an Angel Food cake in the freezer for this quick and easy dessert.

1 small Angel Food cake
4 to 5 oranges (1 cup juice and 1 orange for slicing)
1/3 cup sugar
1 tablespoon, plus 1 teaspoon cornstarch
1 large banana, sliced
2 kiwis, peeled and cut into chunks

In medium saucepan, combine the 1 cup orange juice, sugar and cornstarch. Mix to thoroughly blend and dissolve cornstarch. Bring to a boil; reduce heat and cook until thickened, stirring frequently. Remove from heat; stir in sliced bananas and kiwi. Peel remaining orange; cut into 1/4-inch slices. Cut slices into quarters; add to sauce. Serve over cake slices. Makes 8 servings.

Per serving:

CAL	PRO	CARB	FIB	FAT	SAT	CHOL	SOD
225	4g	53g	2g	<1g	0g	0mg	151mg

APPLE-CRANBERRY CRISP

OVEN 350°

Best saved for a special occasion. The cranberries add a touch of color and flavor. Also good served with a small scoop of frozen yogurt.

8 cups sliced apples (4 to 5 Rome apples)
1 cup fresh or frozen cranberries
1/2 teaspoon cinnamon
3/4 cup flour
1 cup sugar
1/3 cup soft tub margarine

Place apple slices in 11 x 7-inch baking dish sprayed with vegetable cooking spray. Sprinkle cranberries over top. Sprinkle cinnamon over cranberries. Add 3 tablespoons water. In small mixing bowl, combine flour and sugar. Cut in margarine with pastry blender or two knives. Sprinkle over apples. Bake at 350° for 50 to 55 minutes or until light golden. Makes 8 servings.

Per serving:

CAL	PRO	CARB	FIB	FAT	SAT	CHOL	SOD
274	1g	52g	3g	8g	1g	0mg	64mg

BAKED APPLES

OVEN 350°

A light dessert to satisfy the sweet tooth.

Per serving:

1/2 Golden Delicious apple
1 tablespoon light brown sugar
10 raisins
1/2 teaspoon soft tub margarine
1 tablespoon water

Peel apple. Carefully remove core by cutting a "V" in middle of each apple half. Place, cut side up, in baking dish. Sprinkle with brown sugar. Top with raisins and margarine. Add water. Bake at 350° for 20 to 25 minutes or until tender, basting 2 or 3 times with the sauce. Serve hot or warm with sauce. Makes 1 serving.

Per serving:

CAL	PRO	CARB	FIB	FAT	SAT	CHOL	SOD
123	<1g	28g	2g	2g	<1g	0mg	21mg

CANTALOUPE YOGURT DESSERT

A satisfying dessert without all the fat and calories.

Per serving:

1/2 small cantaloupe
1 scoop frozen lowfat vanilla yogurt
1 tablespoon toasted coconut

Remove seeds from center of cantaloupe. Fill with frozen yogurt; sprinkle with coconut. Place on attractive serving plate. Makes 1 serving.

VARIATION: Fill with 1/2 cup fresh raspberries; top with small scoop lemon or pineapple sorbet. Or fill with assorted fresh fruits such as strawberries, bananas, papaya, grapes and blueberries.

Per serving:

CAL	PRO	CARB	FIB	FAT	SAT	CHOL	SOD
196	5g	36g	3g	4g	3g	5mg	69mg

CHEESECAKE DESSERT WITH STRAWBERRIES

CHILL

It's hard to beat this dessert. Easy to make and most attractive when served in your prettiest champagne glasses or dessert dishes.

1 (8-ounce) container Light cream cheese product, softened
1/2 cup sifted powdered sugar
1/4 teaspoon almond extract
2 cups Lite frozen whipped topping, thawed
2 cups fresh strawberries, sliced
2 tablespoons sugar

In mixer bowl, beat cream cheese until light. Add powdered sugar and almond extract. Beat until smooth. Add whipped topping. Mix on low to blend. Spoon into champagne glasses, wine glasses or small dessert dishes. Chill at least 2 hours. While dessert is chilling, combine strawberries with sugar. Chill. To serve, top each dessert with some of the strawberries. Makes 6 servings.

TIP: Can be made a day ahead or frozen.

Per serving:

CAL	PRO	CARB	FIB	FAT	SAT	CHOL	SOD
186	4g	24g	1g	12g	4g	13mg	214mg

CINNAMON PEARS

OVEN 350°

This recipe will satisfy your sweet tooth.

Per serving:

1/2 pear, remove core, but do not peel
1 teaspoon cinnamon sugar
Vanilla ice milk (1/4 cup)

Place pear(s), skin side down, in small baking pan. Sprinkle cinnamon sugar over top. Bake at 350° (325° if using glass) for 35 to 40 minutes or until tender. Serve warm with a small scoop of ice milk. Makes 1 serving.

TIP: If you don't have cinnamon sugar on hand, you can combine 4 teaspoons sugar with 1/4 teaspoon cinnamon (enough for 4 pear halves).

Per half:

CAL	PRO	CARB	FIB	FAT	SAT	CHOL	SOD
120	1g	26g	2g	2g	<1g	4mg	28mg

FROZEN COCONUT BALLS

FREEZE

Coconut is very high in saturated fat. This dessert will let you enjoy the flavor of coconut without destroying your fat allowance for the day.

4 frozen balls made from lowfat vanilla frozen yogurt or ice milk
1/2 cup Angel Flake coconut
1 quart fresh strawberries, sliced
1/4 cup sugar

Make 4 balls using about 1/2 cup yogurt or ice milk. Quickly roll in coconut; freeze until ready to serve. Slice strawberries; toss with just enough sugar to sweeten to taste. Chill until ready to serve. Place frozen balls in serving dishes. Top with strawberries. Enjoy! Makes 4 servings.

Per serving:

CAL	PRO	CARB	FIB	FAT	SAT	CHOL	SOD
247	3g	45g	5g	7g	5g	8mg	80mg

LEMON MOUSSE

CHILL

A light dessert with just 110 calories, but watch the fat grams and enjoy only when you can afford them.

1 (6-ounce) package lemon jello
14 ounces diet 7-Up (1 3/4 cups)
1/4 cup fresh lemon juice
1 (12-ounce) container Lite frozen whipped topping, thawed

Add 2 cups boiling water to lemon jello; stir to dissolve. Add 7-Up and lemon juice. Chill until slightly thickened. Pour mixture into a large mixer bowl. Beat until frothy. Stir in whipped topping until blended. Pour into a large bowl or into small serving dishes or glasses using 3/4 cup per serving. Chill at least an hour. Makes about twelve 3/4 cup servings.

Per serving:

CAL	PRO	CARB	FIB	FAT	SAT	CHOL	SOD
110	5g	16g	0g	6g	0g	0mg	26mg

Ice Cream Sandwiches

FREEZE

Kids will have to compete with the adults for these tiny, but tasty frozen sandwiches.

1 (9-ounce) box chocolate wafer cookies
1/2 gallon vanilla ice milk or frozen lowfat yogurt (round carton, if possible)

Remove paper container from ice milk or frozen yogurt. Cut 1 (1/2-inch) slice. Using a 2-inch cookie or biscuit cutter, cut into small rounds. Place between 2 cookies. Place on cookie sheet to freeze. Continue with remaining ice milk and cookies. The number of sandwiches will depend on how much waste there is and the number of broken cookies in the package. Freeze sandwiches, then place in air tight container or plastic bag.

VARIATION: You can do the same thing with graham cracker squares. Cut ice cream to fit. Vary flavors according to taste.

Per sandwich:

Cal	Pro	Carb	Fib	Fat	Sat	Chol	Sod
70	1g	11g	0g	2g	<1g	2mg	95mg

Graham Cracker Pudding Dessert

CHILL

A nice make ahead dessert.

2 (3.4-ounce) packages instant vanilla pudding
3 cups nonfat milk
1 (8-ounce) container Lite frozen whipped topping, thawed
Graham crackers (about 22 1/2 whole rectangles)
2 tablespoons lightly toasted coconut

In large mixing bowl, combine pudding mix and milk. Stir until slightly thickened. Fold in whipped topping. Place layer of graham crackers to cover bottom of 9 x 13-inch baking dish. Spread with one third of pudding. Add second layer of graham crackers. Spread with one third of pudding. Repeat with remaining crackers and pudding. Sprinkle with toasted coconut. Cover; chill overnight or at least 6 hours before serving. Makes 12 servings.

Per serving:

Cal	Pro	Carb	Fib	Fat	Sat	Chol	Sod
228	4g	43g	<1g	7g	1g	1mg	450mg

LEMON LIGHT DESSERT

CHILL

A simple yet tasty dessert to serve to family and friends. Low-cal too!

1 (3-ounce) package lemon jello
1 cup sugar
1 large lemon (to make 1/4 cup juice and 2 teaspoons lemon peel)
1 (12-ounce) can evaporated skim milk, chilled
1/2 cup, plus 2 tablespoons crushed graham cracker crumbs

Dissolve jello in 3/4 cup boiling water. Stir in sugar, lemon juice and peel. Cool, but do not let thicken. In large mixer bowl, beat milk until light and fluffy. Add jello mixture and beat until blended. Sprinkle graham cracker crumbs in 11 x 7-inch shallow dish sprayed lightly with vegetable cooking spray. Pour lemon mixture into dish. Sprinkle remaining 2 tablespoons crumbs over top. Cover; chill until set. Makes 12 servings.

Per serving:

CAL	PRO	CARB	FIB	FAT	SAT	CHOL	SOD
131	5g	28g	<1g	<1g	<1g	1mg	73mg

FROZEN FRUIT SALAD DESSERT

FREEZE

A sweet-tart fruit salad just perfect on a hot summer day.

4 cups buttermilk
2 cups sugar
1/2 teaspoon almond or vanilla extract
1 (16-ounce) can fruit salad, drained
1 (20-ounce) can crushed pineapple, drained
1/2 cup sliced strawberries

In large mixing bowl, combine buttermilk and sugar; mix well. Stir in remaining ingredients. Pour into 11 x 7-inch baking dish. Cover and freeze until ready to serve. Makes 15 servings.

Per serving:

CAL	PRO	CARB	FIB	FAT	SAT	CHOL	SOD
63	<1g	14g	1g	2g	0g	0mg	<1mg

MANDARIN ORANGE DESSERT

CHILL

Since we can't have our favorite dessert every day, this is a nice substitute.

1 (6-ounce) package orange jello
1 pint Mandarin orange sorbet
1 (11-ounce) can Mandarin oranges, drained thoroughly
1 (16-ounce) can crushed pineapple, drained thoroughly
3/4 cup miniature marshmallows
1 (8-ounce) container Lite frozen whipped topping, thawed

In large mixing bowl, combine jello with 2 cups boiling water, stirring until completely dissolved. Stir in sorbet until melted. Chill until thickened, about 30 minutes. Add oranges, pineapple and marshmallows. Fold in whipped topping. Pour into 9 x 13-inch dish. Cover; chill until set. Cut into squares to serve. Makes 15 servings.

VARIATION: Add 2 large bananas, sliced.

Per serving:

CAL	PRO	CARB	FIB	FAT	SAT	CHOL	SOD
140	4g	22g	<1g	4g	0g	0mg	22mg

FROZEN YOGURT WITH AMARETTO

A great company dessert.

Per serving:

1 scoop frozen low-fat yogurt
1 tablespoon Amaretto liqueur
2 tablespoon Lite frozen whipped topping, thawed
1 tablespoon toasted Angel Flake coconut

Place scoop of yogurt in champagne glass or small dessert dish. Spoon Amaretto over top. Top with whipped topping. Sprinkle with coconut. Makes 1 serving.

Per serving:

CAL	PRO	CARB	FIB	FAT	SAT	CHOL	SOD
205	3g	27g	1g	7g	4g	5mg	62mg

RASPBERRY COOKIE DESSERT

OVEN 350°

Served warm with a scoop of ice milk or sherbet this makes a wonderful no cholesterol dessert. You can also cut it into small cookie-size squares.

1/2 cup firmly packed light brown sugar, packed
1/2 cup soft tub margarine
1 cup flour
1 cup old fashioned rolled oats
1/4 teaspoon baking soda
2/3 cup seedless raspberry jam

In mixer bowl, beat sugar and margarine until mixed. Add flour, oats, and baking soda. Beat until well mixed. Spray 8 x 8-inch baking dish generously with vegetable cooking spray. Pat 2 cups of mixture evenly into pan. Spread with jam. Crumble remaining mixture over top. Press gently into the jam. Bake at 350° (325° if using glass) for 30 to 35 minutes or until lightly browned. Mixture will appear quite soft, but will firm up somewhat when cooled. Makes 8 servings.

Per serving:

CAL	PRO	CARB	FIB	FAT	SAT	CHOL	SOD
319	3g	50g	2g	12g	2g	0mg	129mg

STRAWBERRY DESSERT

CHILL

Keep ingredients on hand for an easy dessert.

1 (6-ounce) package strawberry jello
2 cups boiling water
2 (10-ounce) packages frozen strawberries with juice, thawed
1 (8-ounce) container Lite frozen whipped topping, thawed
1 (12-ounce) purchased Angel Food cake, torn into very small pieces

In large mixing bowl, combine jello and boiling water; stir to completely dissolve. Stir in strawberries. Refrigerate until thickened, about 45 minutes. Fold in whipped topping. Carefully fold in cake pieces. Pour into 9 x 13-inch dish. Cover and refrigerate until firm. Makes 15 servings.

Per serving:

CAL	PRO	CARB	FIB	FAT	SAT	CHOL	SOD
203	7g	42g	1g	4g	0g	0mg	120mg

ORANGE CREAM CHEESE DESSERT

CHILL

Very similar to Orange Cheesecake Pie, but even lower in fat and calories. You may wish to make half the recipe since this does make a lot.

2 (8-ounce) containers Light cream cheese product, softened
1 cup sugar
1/3 cup fresh orange juice
1 teaspoon grated orange peel
1 (12-ounce) container Lite frozen whipped topping, thawed
3 tablespoons toasted coconut

In large mixer bowl, beat cream cheese until smooth. Add sugar, orange juice and peel; mix until well blended and smooth. Add whipped topping; mix well. Spoon into 10 small dessert dishes or wine glasses. Sprinkle with coconut. Chill at least 2 hours. Makes 10 servings.

Per serving:

CAL	PRO	CARB	FIB	FAT	SAT	CHOL	SOD
252	5g	33g	<1g	16g	5g	16mg	261mg

PINEAPPLE ORANGE DESSERT

A quick light dessert for after a hearty meal.

1 medium large orange, peeled, cut into 4 slices
4 slices canned pineapple (or use fresh)
1 tablespoon Cointreau
8 tablespoons Lite frozen whipped topping, thawed
1 teaspoon grated orange peel

Place an orange and pineapple slice on each of four small serving plates. Drizzle Cointreau over fruit. Top each serving with 2 tablespoons whipped topping. Sprinkle with grated peel. Makes 4 servings.

Per serving:

CAL	PRO	CARB	FIB	FAT	SAT	CHOL	SOD
63	<1g	14g	1g	2g	0g	0mg	<1mg

MIXED FRUIT DESSERT

A refreshing light dessert for a hot summer evening.

1 cup watermelon balls
1 cup cantaloupe balls
1 cup seedless green grapes
1 cup Bing cherries, pitted and halved
4 scoops of lemon sherbet (about 1/4 cup each)

Combine fruit in medium bowl. Spoon into small serving dishes; top with scoop of lemon sherbet. Makes 4 servings.

Per serving:

CAL	PRO	CARB	FIB	FAT	SAT	CHOL	SOD
149	2g	34g	1g	2g	<1g	4mg	27mg

QUICK AND EASY FRUIT COBBLER

OVEN 350°

Very good with fresh or canned fruit.

1/2 cup soft tub margarine
1 cup flour
1 cup sugar
2 teaspoons baking powder
3/4 cup 1% milk
1 quart fresh berries or 1 (16-ounce) can sliced peaches, drained

Heat oven to 350°. Place margarine in 8 x 8-inch baking dish and put in oven to melt. Combine flour, sugar and baking powder. Add milk to melted margarine. With a fork, stir in flour mixture until smooth. Top with fruit. Bake 50 to 60 minutes or until golden and cooked through. Makes 6 servings.

Per serving:

CAL	PRO	CARB	FIB	FAT	SAT	CHOL	SOD
352	3g	51g	<1g	15g	3g	1mg	252mg

QUICK PEAR DELIGHT

Sweet enough to satisfy your sweet tooth.

Per serving:

2 canned pear halves, drained thoroughly
2 tablespoons Lite frozen whipped topping, thawed
1 teaspoon finely chopped walnuts

Place pears in dessert dish. Top with whipped topping. Sprinkle with walnuts. Makes 1 serving.

Per serving:

CAL	PRO	CARB	FIB	FAT	SAT	CHOL	SOD
109	1g	22g	2g	3g	<1g	0mg	6mg

MANDARIN ORANGE DELIGHT

CHILL

Kids love this! It is light and easy for them to eat.

1 (8-ounce) container lowfat Mandarin orange yogurt
1 cup Lite frozen whipped topping, thawed
1 (11-ounce) can Mandarin oranges, drained thoroughly

In small bowl, combine yogurt and whipped topping. Gently stir in oranges. Cover and chill until ready to serve. Makes 4 servings.

Per serving:

CAL	PRO	CARB	FIB	FAT	SAT	CHOL	SOD
113	3g	21g	1g	4g	<1g	2mg	36mg

QUICK ANGEL DESSERT

Per serving:

1 slice Angel Food cake
1/2 cup sliced fresh strawberries
2 tablespoons Lite frozen whipped topping, thawed

Place cake on attractive serving dish. Top with strawberries and whipped topping.

Per serving:

CAL	PRO	CARB	FIB	FAT	SAT	CHOL	SOD
180	4g	39g	2g	2g	0g	0mg	150mg

GRAHAM CRACKER CRUST

OVEN 350°

$1^1/_4$ cups graham cracker crumbs
2 tablespoons sugar
$^1/_4$ cup soft tub margarine, melted

Combine ingredients until well mixed. Press evenly into bottom and sides of 9-inch pie pan. Bake at 350° for 10 minutes. Let cool before filling. Makes 1 pie crust.

Per $^1/_8$ serving:

CAL	PRO	CARB	FIB	FAT	SAT	CHOL	SOD
134	2g	17g	<1g	7g	1g	0mg	173mg

PRETZEL PIE CRUST

OVEN 350°

$1^1/_3$ cups crushed pretzels
6 tablespoons soft tub margarine, melted
$1^1/_2$ tablespoons sugar

Combine ingredients; mix well to blend. Pat into 9-inch pie pan. Bake at 350° for 10 minutes. Cool. Makes 1 crust.

TIP: When doubled, this recipe makes a good base for desserts and jello salads, using a 9 x 13-inch dish.

Per $^1/_8$ serving:

CAL	PRO	CARB	FIB	FAT	SAT	CHOL	SOD
141	1g	14g	<1g	9g	2g	0mg	299mg

MERINGUE SHELL

OVEN 275°

Meringue shells are convenient to use and contain no fat.

3 egg whites
$^1/_4$ teaspoon cream of tartar
$^1/_4$ teaspoon vanilla extract
$^2/_3$ cup sugar

In large mixer bowl, beat egg whites, cream of tartar and vanilla until foamy. Gradually add small amounts of sugar, beating until dissolved and stiff peaks form. Lightly oil a 9-inch pie pan, (do not use vegetable cooking spray). Spread meringue in pan, building up sides to form a shell. Bake at 275° for 1 hour and 15 minutes or until very light color and dry in appearance. Let cool; carefully remove from pan, if desired. Makes 1 pie shell.

Per $^1/_8$ serving:

CAL	PRO	CARB	FIB	FAT	SAT	CHOL	SOD
71	1g	17g	0g	0g	0g	0mg	21mg

PIE CRUST

OVEN 450°

This recipe uses oil and is a very good substitute for the pie crusts we have always enjoyed.

1 1/3 cups flour
1/4 teaspoon salt
1/3 cup Canola oil
3 tablespoons ice cold water

Combine flour and salt in small bowl. Combine oil and water. Add to flour. Stir with fork until mixed. This is somewhat dry; you will have to use your hands to form into a ball. On lightly floured surface, roll into a circle 1-inch larger than inverted pie pan. Fold over rolling pin and place in pan. Press to fit, folding edges under to form a rim. If a baked crust is desired, prick all over with a fork and bake at 450° for 12 to 14 minutes or until lightly browned (cooking time may vary according to type of pan used and your oven). Let cool.

Per 1/8 serving:

CAL	PRO	CARB	FIB	FAT	SAT	CHOL	SOD
156	2g	16g	<1g	9g	<1g	0mg	67mg

FRUIT RIPPLE PIE

FREEZE

You may substitute strawberries for the raspberries.

1 (9-inch) baked pie crust
1 cup fresh raspberries
1 pint raspberry sorbet
1 quart ice milk, softened
1 tablespoon toasted sliced almonds

In large bowl, carefully fold raspberries into sorbet. Fold ice milk into sorbet mixture, stirring lightly to achieve marbled effect. Spoon into pie crust. Freeze. Cover with foil until ready to serve. Sprinkle pie with almonds and serve. Makes 8 servings.

TIP: If fresh raspberries aren't available, use a 10-ounce package frozen raspberries, thawed and drained.

Per serving:

CAL	PRO	CARB	FIB	FAT	SAT	CHOL	SOD
263	4g	31g	1g	10g	2g	6mg	99mg

STRAWBERRY PIE

CHILL

1 (9-inch) baked pie shell
1 cup sugar
3 tablespoons cornstarch
3 tablespoons strawberry jello (powder)
3 cups fresh whole strawberries

Place sugar in small saucepan. Combine cornstarch with 1/4 cup cold water, stirring until smooth. Add to saucepan along with 3/4 cup water. Cook over medium low heat until thickened, stirring frequently. Add jello; stir to dissolve. Line pie shell with strawberries, stem end down, filling in where necessary with smaller berries. Pour sauce over top. Chill until set. Makes 8 servings.

Per serving:

CAL	PRO	CARB	FIB	FAT	SAT	CHOL	SOD
284	4g	47g	<1g	9g	<1g	0mg	77mg

SORBET MERINGUE PIE

FREEZE

1 (9-inch) meringue shell (see page 68)
3 pints sorbet (any combination of flavors)
2 tablespoons chocolate sauce

Shape sorbet into small balls; arrange in pie shell. Drizzle with chocolate sauce. Freeze until ready to serve. Makes 8 servings.

Per serving:

CAL	PRO	CARB	FIB	FAT	SAT	CHOL	SOD
335	3g	47g	<1g	2g	1g	1mg	51mg

STRAWBERRY-RASPBERRY PIE

CHILL

A favorite with kids. They love the bright red color.

1 (9-inch) pretzel pie crust, baked (see page 68)
1 (3-ounce) package raspberry jello
1 pint vanilla ice milk
1 1/2 cups sliced fresh strawberries
3/4 cup Lite frozen whipped topping, thawed

Dissolve jello in 1 1/4 cups boiling water. Add ice milk, stirring to dissolve. Chill until thickened. Add strawberries. Pour into pie shell. Chill until set. Top each serving with 2 tablespoons whipped topping. Makes 8 servings.

Per serving:

CAL	PRO	CARB	FIB	FAT	SAT	CHOL	SOD
254	2g	32g	1g	12g	3g	4mg	343mg

ORANGE CHEESECAKE PIE

CHILL

This delicious dessert can be made ahead. If frozen, thaw before serving.

1 (9-inch) graham cracker crust (page 68)
2 (8-ounce) packages Light cream cheese product, softened
1 cup sugar
1/2 cup fresh orange juice
1 (12-ounce) container Lite frozen whipped topping, thawed

In large mixer bowl, beat cream cheese until smooth. Beat in sugar. Gradually add orange juice to cream cheese mixture, beating until smooth. Add whipped topping; mix until well blended. Pour into pie crust. Chill at least two hours. Makes 10 servings.

TIP: The pie will be quite full. If using purchased graham cracker crust this recipe will make 2 pies.

Per 1/10 serving:

CAL	PRO	CARB	FIB	FAT	SAT	CHOL	SOD
352	6g	46g	<1g	21g	6g	16mg	395mg

Cook's Tip

Planning ahead will make it a lot easier for you to stick to your allowed daily fat grams.

Brunch & Lunch

OATMEAL WITH PINEAPPLE

TOP OF STOVE

1 (8-ounce) can pineapple tidbits with juice
1 cup old-fashioned rolled oats
4 teaspoons firmly packed light brown sugar
1/4 teaspoon cinnamon
1/3 cup raisins
3/4 cup nonfat milk

In medium saucepan, combine pineapple and juice with 1 1/2 cups water. Bring to a boil. Add rolled oats, brown sugar, cinnamon and raisins. Cook 5 minutes. Remove from heat. Cover; let stand about 5 minutes. Spoon into serving bowls; top each with 3 tablespoons milk. Makes 4 servings.

Per serving:

CAL	PRO	CARB	FIB	FAT	SAT	CHOL	SOD
181	5g	39g	4g	1g	<1g	<1mg	28mg

DATE OATMEAL

TOP OF STOVE

Add a glass of tomato juice and fresh fruit for a rich and satisfying breakfast with almost no fat.

1 cup apple juice
1 cup water
1 cup quick-cooking oats
1/4 cup finely chopped dates (about 3 large)
1/8 teaspoon cinnamon
3/4 cup nonfat milk

In medium saucepan, bring apple juice and water to a boil. Stir in oats. Cook 1 minute. Stir in dates and cinnamon. Let stand 4 to 5 minutes. Pour 1/4 cup milk over each serving. Makes 3 servings.

Per serving:

CAL	PRO	CARB	FIB	FAT	SAT	CHOL	SOD
203	7g	41g	4g	2g	<1g	1mg	41mg

Onion Omelet for Two

TOP OF STOVE

If you prefer individual omelets, use half the ingredients for each omelet and use a smaller pan.

1 teaspoon Canola oil
1/2 cup finely chopped onion
1 cup egg substitute
Salt and pepper (optional)

Heat oil in 9-inch non-stick skillet. Add onion; cook until soft, stirring frequently. Add egg substitute. Cook over medium heat, lifting gently to allow uncooked portion to flow underneath. When bottom is cooked, turn and finish cooking (this doesn't take long). If omelet is difficult to turn, place under boiler and finish cooking. Cut in half to serve. Makes 2 servings.

Per serving:

Cal	Pro	Carb	Fib	Fat	Sat	Chol	Sod
91	11g	7g	<1g	2g	<1g	0mg	161mg

Buttermilk Pancakes

TOP OF STOVE

The flour-buttermilk mixture should stand over night.

1 cup flour
1 cup buttermilk
1/4 cup egg substitute
1 teaspoon baking soda
1/4 teaspoon salt

Combine flour and buttermilk. Cover; let stand overnight. When ready to cook, stir in remaining ingredients. Spray non-stick skillet or griddle with vegetable cooking spray. Heat over medium heat. When hot add batter. Cook pancakes, until bubbles form on top; turn and cook other side. Makes 6 pancakes.

Per pancake:

Cal	Pro	Carb	Fib	Fat	Sat	Chol	Sod
97	4g	18g	<1g	<1g	<1g	1mg	282mg

SWEDISH PANCAKES

TOP OF STOVE

Serve with syrup, fresh fruit, powdered sugar or apple sauce.

1 cup nonfat milk
1 cup flour
2 tablespoons sugar
1 cup egg substitute

In medium mixing bowl, combine all the ingredients, mixing until smooth. Heat an 8 or 9-inch non-stick skillet, sprayed with vegetable cooking spray, over medium heat. Pour about 1/4 cup batter into pan, tilting pan to coat bottom. Cook until slightly dry on top; turn and quickly cook other side. Roll pancake; turn out of pan. Makes 10 pancakes.

Per pancake:

CAL	PRO	CARB	FIB	FAT	SAT	CHOL	SOD
74	4g	14g	<1g	<1g	0g	<1mg	45mg

FRENCH TOAST

TOP OF STOVE

1 egg white
1/4 cup egg substitute
1/4 cup nonfat milk
1/4 teaspoon vanilla or almond extract
Dash cinnamon
6 slices bread (French or Italian)

Combine first 5 ingredients; mix well to blend. Spray large non-stick skillet with vegetable cooking spray. Heat over medium heat. Dip bread in egg mixture. Brown on both sides. Makes 3 servings.

Per serving:

CAL	PRO	CARB	FIB	FAT	SAT	CHOL	SOD
223	10g	40g	1g	2g	<1g	2mg	462mg

MAPLE SYRUP WITH ALMOND

TOP OF STOVE

The almond adds a nice touch to an old favorite.

3/4 cup sugar
1/4 cup firmly packed light brown sugar
1/8 teaspoon Mapeline (flavoring)
1/4 teaspoon almond, rum or vanilla extract
1/2 cup water

Combine ingredients in medium saucepan, stirring to blend. Bring to a boil; reduce heat and simmer, stirring frequently, until sugar dissolves. Makes 1 cup.

Per tablespoon:

CAL	PRO	CARB	FIB	FAT	SAT	CHOL	SOD
49	0g	13g	0g	0g	0g	0mg	1mg

LEMON SYRUP

TOP OF STOVE

A light lemon syrup to serve with waffles, French toast and oven pancakes.

1/2 cup sugar
1 tablespoon cornstarch, plus 1 teaspoon
1 lemon (1 teaspoon grated peel and 2 tablespoons juice)
1 teaspoon soft tub margarine

In small saucepan, combine sugar and cornstarch; mix well. Add water; stir to mix (this is easily done with a whisk). Bring to a boil; reduce heat and cook until thickened, stirring frequently. Add lemon peel, juice and margarine. Keep warm until ready to serve or cover and chill. Makes 1 1/4 cups.

Per tablespoon:

CAL	PRO	CARB	FIB	FAT	SAT	CHOL	SOD
23	0g	6g	0g	<1g	0g	0mg	2mg

ORANGE ALMOND SYRUP

TOP OF STOVE

Delicious over French toast, pancakes, waffles and vanilla ice milk.

3/4 cup honey
1 teaspoon soft tub margarine
1 orange (1/4 cup juice and 1 teaspoon grated peel)
1/4 teaspoon almond extract

Combine ingredients in small saucepan. Heat until ingredients are blended. Serve warm or store in refrigerator. Makes 1 1/4 cups.

Per tablespoon:

CAL	PRO	CARB	FIB	FAT	SAT	CHOL	SOD
42	0g	11g	0g	<1g	0g	0mg	2mg

TURKEY SAUSAGE CASSEROLE

TOP OF STOVE
CHILL
OVEN 350°

Assemble day ahead or several hours ahead and refrigerate.

1 (16-ounce) package turkey breakfast sausage
8 ounces French bread, cut into cubes
$2^1/_2$ cups nonfat milk
2 (8-ounce) cartons egg substitute
1 cup (4-ounces) Lite Mozzarella cheese, shredded
1 cup (4-ounces) reduced fat Cheddar cheese, shredded

Separate turkey into small pieces and drop in non-stick skillet. Cook over medium heat until browned, stirring frequently. Drain off liquid. Place bread cubes in 9x13-inch baking dish sprayed with non-stick vegetable cooking spray. Top with sausage. Combine milk and egg substitute. Pour over meat. Combine cheese to mix. Sprinkle over top. Cover with foil; chill several hours or overnight. Remove foil; bake at 350° for 35 to 40 minutes or until golden and most of the liquid is absorbed. Makes 8 servings.

Per serving:

CAL	PRO	CARB	FIB	FAT	SAT	CHOL	SOD
291	26g	23g	<1g	10g	5g	51mg	582mg

Cook's Tip
Bread Serving Bowl

An attractive way to serve chicken legs or chicken salad.

1 large round loaf unsliced French or sourdough bread
Melted margarine
Basil or oregano

Cut a 1-inch top off bread. Remove most of the bread, leaving about a 1-inch shell. Spread inside of the bowl with margarine. Sprinkle lightly with basil or oregano. Bake at 375° for 10 to 12 minutes or until bread is lightly browned and crisp. Place on serving plate; fill with chicken legs, wings or chicken salad. After filling is served, the bread bowl can be eaten. Holds 6 to 8 pieces of chicken, depending on the size of the bread.

CHICKEN NOODLE SOUP

TOP OF STOVE

7 cups chicken broth
3 medium carrots, cut into 1/8-inch slices
1/2 cup sliced celery
3/4 cup frozen peas
1 cup (6-ounces) cooked chicken, cubed
4 ounces spaghetti noodles, cooked

In large saucepan or pot, combine broth, carrots and celery. Bring to a boil; reduce heat and simmer until vegetables are crisp tender, about 6 to 8 minutes. Add peas, chicken and cooked noodles. Cook until heated through. Makes 10 cups.

Per 1 cup serving:

CAL	PRO	CARB	FIB	FAT	SAT	CHOL	SOD
113	9g	14g	<1g	2g	na	na	726mg

CHICKEN-VEGETABLESOUP

TOP OF STOVE

A small amount of ground chicken goes a long way in this hearty vegetable soup.

1/2 pound lean ground chicken
1 cup chopped onion
3 cups sliced carrots (about 6 medium)
4 cups diced potatoes
1 (1 pound 12-ounce) can tomatoes, with juice
Salt and pepper to taste

Drop small amounts of ground chicken in medium non-stick skillet. Add onion. Cook until chicken is brown and onion is soft. In large pot or Dutch oven, add carrots, potatoes and tomatoes with juice (cut tomatoes into smaller pieces). Add chicken mixture. Stir in 3 1/2 cups water. Bring to a boil; reduce heat and simmer about 1 hour or until vegetables are tender. Makes 8 cups.

Per 1 cup serving:

CAL	PRO	CARB	FIB	FAT	SAT	CHOL	SOD
160	3g	28g	5g	3g	na	19mg	301mg

LIGHT CHICKEN SOUP

TOP OF STOVE

6 cups chicken broth
1/2 cup (3-ounces) cooked chicken, cut into slivers
3 ounces vermicelli noodles, broken into fourths
1/2 cup green onion, sliced into 1-inch pieces

Combine broth and chicken in large saucepan. Bring to a boil; add vermicelli and cook about 7 minutes, until almost done. Add onion and cook until noodles are tender. Makes 6 cups.

Per 1 cup serving:

CAL	PRO	CARB	FIB	FAT	SAT	CHOL	SOD
124	9g	16g	<1g	3g	na	na	1008mg

CHICKEN BROTH

TOP OF STOVE

Chicken broth will keep a couple of days in the refrigerator or can be frozen.

4 to 5 pounds chicken backs and wings
2 large onions, quartered, separated
3 carrots, sliced
3 celery stalks, cut into 2-inch pieces
Salt and pepper to taste

Place ingredients in large pot. Add water to cover. Bring to a boil; skim off foam. Simmer, partially covered, 2 to 3 hours. Taste for flavor. If broth is flavorful enough for you it is done. The more concentrated the broth, the more flavor it will have. Remove chicken and vegetables. Strain broth. Add salt and pepper to taste. Refrigerate to chill. Lift off fat. Makes 8 cups.

We do not have capabilities to analyze this recipe. It is however, very low in fat.

CREAM OF POTATO SOUP

TOP OF STOVE

This is delicious served on a night you choose to have a meatless dinner. For adults use 2 cup servings. Add toasted French bread, a large tossed green salad and Angel Food cake with sliced strawberries.

5 cups potatoes, peeled and diced into 1/2-inch cubes
1/3 cup finely chopped onion
3/4 cup dry nonfat milk
2 tablespoons cornstarch
1/2 cup frozen peas
Salt and pepper to taste

Place potatoes and onion in large saucepan. Add 1 1/2 cups water. Cook over medium heat until potatoes are tender, about 10 to 15 minutes. (Do not over cook or potatoes will turn into mush.) Combine dry milk and cornstarch. Add 1 cup water; add to potatoes. Stir in peas. Cook, stirring occasionally, until thickened. Add salt and pepper to taste. Makes four 1-cup servings.

Per serving:

CAL	PRO	CARB	FIB	FAT	SAT	CHOL	SOD
199	8g	42g	3g	<1g	<1g	2mg	151mg

POTATO SOUP

TOP OF STOVE

A large bowl of potato soup is good on those days when you indulge in your favorite steak, fettucine or dessert. Serve with hard rolls.

1/3 cup chopped onion
1/4 cup finely chopped green pepper
4 medium potatoes, about 3 1/2 cups, cut into small cubes
Salt and pepper to taste
2 tablespoons flour
1 cup nonfat milk

Place onion and green pepper in medium saucepan. Add about 1/4 cup water. Cook until vegetables are soft. Add cubed potatoes and water to cover, about 1 to 1 1/2 cups. Cook 10 minutes or until potatoes are soft, but not mushy. Combine flour with 1/4 cup water. Stir into potato mixture. Add milk. Cook until thickened and heated through. Makes 4 cups.

Per 1 cup serving:

CAL	PRO	CARB	FIB	FAT	SAT	CHOL	SOD
160	5g	35g	3g	<1g	<1g	1mg	94mg

SAUSAGE-POTATO SOUP

TOP OF STOVE

A hearty full-meal soup. If you want to save your fat grams for another meal, omit meat.

1 (8 ounce) package frozen turkey sausage, thawed
1 (28-ounce) can tomatoes, with juice
3 cups cubed potatoes
2 cups chopped onion
1 (15¹/4-ounce) can light kidney beans, drained
1¹/2 cups frozen peas

In medium non-stick skillet, crumble sausage into very small chunks. Cook over medium heat until browned and cooked through. Drain off liquid. Put in large pot or Dutch oven. Add tomatoes (tomatoes should be cut into small pieces). Add potatoes, onions and kidney beans. Stir in peas. Add 3 cups water. Bring to a boil; reduce heat and simmer about 45 minutes or until potatoes are tender. Makes 11 cups.

TIP: If you prefer not to use sausage, you can add ³/4 pound browned ground chicken. In this case you may wish to add a little salt and pepper for added flavor.

Per 1 cup serving:

CAL	PRO	CARB	FIB	FAT	SAT	CHOL	SOD
144	7g	23g	3g	3g	<1g	13mg	255mg

SPLIT PEA SOUP

TOP OF STOVE

Nutritious and filling with a minimum of fat. Serve with Whole Wheat Muffins or toasted bagels and tossed green salad.

1 cup (6-ounces) finely diced cooked chicken
1 (16-ounce) package split peas, rinsed and drained
³/4 cup finely diced carrots
3 cups cubed potatoes
8 cups chicken broth
Salt and pepper to taste

In a large pot, combine all the ingredients except salt and pepper. Bring to a boil, reduce heat. Cover and simmer about 45 minutes or until vegetables are tender and soup has thickened. Makes 11 cups.

Per 1 cup serving:

CAL	PRO	CARB	FIB	FAT	SAT	CHOL	SOD
226	17g	35g	7g	3g	na	na	751mg

MINESTRONE SOUP

TOP OF STOVE

1 (14.5-ounce) can Italian stewed tomatoes
1 (15-ounce) can light kidney beans, drained
1 (10-ounce) package frozen mixed vegetables
1/2 cup chopped onion
3/4 cup small elbow macaroni, uncooked
Salt and pepper to taste

Cut stewed tomatoes into smaller pieces; add to large pot along with the juice. Add kidney beans, frozen vegetables and onion. Stir in seven cups water. Bring to a boil; reduce heat and simmer 45 minutes. Add macaroni (it may be necessary to raise to medium heat); cook 8 to 10 minutes or until tender. Makes 10 cups.

Per 1 cup serving:

CAL	PRO	CARB	FIB	FAT	SAT	CHOL	SOD
106	4g	22g	2g	<1g	0g	0mg	224mg

HAM AND LIMA BEAN SOUP

TOP OF STOVE

2 cups dried baby Lima beans
2 bay leaves
1 medium onion, cut into wedges
1/3 cup finely chopped or cubed ham
Salt and pepper to taste

Wash beans; remove the bad ones. Place in large pot; add 8 cups water. Cover; soak overnight. When ready to cook, add bay leaves, onion and ham. Bring to a boil, reduce heat and simmer 1 1/2 to 2 hours or until beans are tender, adding more water if necessary. Season to taste with salt and pepper. Makes 8 cups.

Per 1 cup serving:

CAL	PRO	CARB	FIB	FAT	SAT	CHOL	SOD
154	9g	28g	11g	<1g	<1g	3mg	150mg

Cook's Tip

Fat rises to the surface of soups and broths and can be skimmed. Even easier, if soup can be chilled, and time allows, the fat will solidify and can be easily removed.

ORIENTAL SOUP

MARINATE
TOP OF STOVE

It is hard to find a 1-pound London Broil or flank steak (the recommended weight for 4 servings). Use some of the remaining meat for this flavorful and quick soup. Very low in fat and calories.

4 ounces London Broil or flank steak
1 teaspoon cornstarch
1 teaspoon sugar
2 teaspoons reduced sodium soy sauce
2 cups beef broth
2 cups Bok Choy, sliced thin (use both white and green part)

Trim fat from meat. Cut beef lengthwise (with the grain) into 1 1/2 to 2-inch strips. Cut each strip across the grain into 1/8-inch slices (this will make thin narrow strips of meat). In small bowl, combine cornstarch, sugar and soy sauce; stir until smooth. Add meat stirring to coat. Cover and chill 30 minutes to marinate. When ready to serve, in medium saucepan, bring broth to a boil. Add Bok Choy; cook about 1 1/2 to 2 minutes until just crisp tender. Add meat; cook about 1 minute. Makes 4 cups.

Per 1 cup serving:

CAL	PRO	CARB	FIB	FAT	SAT	CHOL	SOD
72	8g	2g	<1g	2g	1g	14mg	511mg

ORIENTAL SHRIMP SOUP

TOP OF STOVE

4 cups chicken broth
1/4 cup shredded carrot
2 cups coarsely chopped Bok Choy (use both white and green part)
1/4 cup finely chopped water chestnuts
2 ounces sliced cooked mushrooms
2 ounces tiny cooked shrimp

In large saucepan, bring chicken broth to a boil. Add carrots, Bok Choy, water chestnuts and mushrooms. Bring to a boil; reduce heat and simmer 3 to 4 minutes or until Bok choy is just crisp tender. Add shrimp and heat through. Makes 4 cups.

Per 1 cup serving:

CAL	PRO	CARB	FIB	FAT	SAT	CHOL	SOD
63	6g	5g	1g	3g	na	na	1054mg

BREAD BOWL SANDWICH

It's fun to do something a little different. A great way to make sandwiches for a picnic.

Sandwich for two:

1 (5-6-inch) round loaf unsliced sourdough bread
1 tablespoon reduced calorie mayonnaise
3 ounces thinly sliced deli turkey
1 small plum tomato, sliced lengthwise
Alfalfa sprouts or lettuce

Cut a 1 to 1½-inch slice off top of loaf. Remove bread from center, leaving a ¼-inch shell. Spread inside of shell with mayonnaise. Arrange folded slices of turkey on bottom of shell. Top with tomato slices, then alfalfa sprouts or lettuce. Replace top. Cut in half to serve. Makes 2 servings.

TIP: You can vary the type of bread and the size of the loaf as well as the filling.

Per serving:

CAL	PRO	CARB	FIB	FAT	SAT	CHOL	SOD
185	17g	23g	1g	3g	<1g	39mg	93mg

CANADIAN BACON MELTS

BROIL

Per serving:

½ English muffin
Mustard
2 thin slices Canadian bacon
1 thin slice tomato
Basil
½ slice Lite Swiss cheese

Spread muffin with small amount of mustard. Top with Canadian bacon and tomato slice. Sprinkle lightly with basil. Place on small baking pan; broil until heated through. Top with cheese; broil until melted. Makes 1 serving:

Per serving:

CAL	PRO	CARB	FIB	FAT	SAT	CHOL	SOD
205	18g	15g	<1g	7g	3g	37mg	976mg

LOW-CAL TOMATO SANDWICH

Enjoy this sandwich when tomatoes are in season.

Per sandwich:

2 slices sourdough bread
1 tablespoon reduced calorie mayonnaise
4 (1/4-inch) slices tomato
Alfalfa sprouts

Spread bread with mayonnaise. Top with tomato and desired amount of sprouts. Makes 1 sandwich.

Per sandwich:

CAL	PRO	CARB	FIB	FAT	SAT	CHOL	SOD
137	4g	21g	1g	5g	1g	5mg	127mg

OPEN-FACE GRILLED CHICKEN SANDWICH

TOP OF STOVE

Per sandwich:

1 chicken breast half, skinned and boned
1/2 teaspoon soft tub margarine, melted
1 teaspoon honey
1 teaspoon reduced sodium soy sauce
1 slice French bread, toasted
Lettuce

Pat chicken dry; trim off all fat. Place between waxed paper. Pound lightly until even and about 1/4-inch thick. Combine margarine, honey and soy sauce; brush on chicken. Place in heated non-stick skillet sprayed with vegetable cooking spray. Cook 2 to 3 minutes per side or until cooked through. Watch carefully as the honey has a tendency to burn. Place lettuce on toasted bread; top with chicken. Makes 1 serving.

VARIATION: Top chicken with a pineapple slice or garnish sandwich with sliced tomatoes and pickle spears.

Per sandwich:

CAL	PRO	CARB	FIB	FAT	SAT	CHOL	SOD
300	30g	26g	1g	6g	1g	73mg	446mg

CHICKEN SALAD SANDWICH CAKE

CHILL

Perfect for a holiday, bridal shower or luncheon. Make day ahead.

4 cups finely diced cooked chicken breast
1/2 cup finely chopped celery
1/2 cup chopped pecans
3/4 to 1 cup reduced calorie mayonnaise
2 (24-ounce) loaves unsliced whole wheat bread (13x4 1/2-inches)
1 (12-ounce) container Light cream cheese product, room temperature

Combine first 4 ingredients. Cover and chill to blend flavors. Cut bread into 1/2-inch lengthwise slices (ask your bakery to do this for you, if possible). Trim crusts to make 5 rectangles about 10 1/2x4-inches in size. Because of the shape of the loaves, you will have a lot of waste in order to get 5 rectangles of the same size. Divide salad into 5 equal portions and spread evenly on bread. Starting at the narrow end of one slice, roll up like a jelly-roll. Place roll at end of another slice, matching evenly. Press slightly. Continue rolling as for jelly-roll. Repeat with remaining slices. Place flat side up on serving dish. Use toothpicks at end of roll, if necessary. Trim top to make even. In mixer bowl, lightly whip cream cheese until smooth. Frost sides and top. Cover (a cake plate with cover is handy). Chill until ready to serve. Slice into wedges. Makes 8 servings.

TIP: Use a dark-type bread. The contrast between the dark bread and the light chicken salad makes for more attractive slices. The "cake" can be decorated any number of ways. For a bridal shower you can decorate with fresh tiny pink rosebuds and baby's breath. For a summer luncheon decorate with fresh strawberries or raspberries.

Per serving:

CAL	PRO	CARB	FIB	FAT	SAT	CHOL	SOD
461	32g	33g	5g	24g	7g	81mg	767mg

SPECIAL TURKEY SANDWICH

2 slices sourdough bread
1 ounce (about 1 tablespoon) Light cream cheese product, softened
2 tablespoons cranberry sauce
2 ounces sliced cooked turkey
Lettuce leaves

Spread one side of each bread slice with cream cheese. Spread with cranberry sauce. Add turkey and lettuce. Makes 1 sandwich.

Per sandwich:

CAL	PRO	CARB	FIB	FAT	SAT	CHOL	SOD
275	24g	34g	2g	6g	3g	59mg	213mg

GRINDERS

OVEN 400°

Tired of the same old sandwiches. These are a family favorite and quick to make.

4 sourdough rolls (hero type) about 6 to 8 inches in length
1/4 cup reduced calorie mayonnaise
12 thin slices Canadian bacon
1 (8-ounce) can pineapple tidbits, drained
3 ounces Lite Mozzarella cheese, shredded
2 cups coarsely shredded or cut lettuce

Separate rolls. Place cut side up on baking sheet. Bake at 400° for 2 to 3 minutes or until bread is lightly toasted. Remove from oven and spread with mayonnaise. Top each of 4 halves with 3 slices Canadian bacon. Top each with some of the pineapple. Sprinkle with cheese. Place the 4 halves in oven; bake 2 to 3 minutes or until cheese is melted. Remove from oven; top each with some of the lettuce. Top with remaining bread halves. Serve hot. Makes 4 sandwiches.

TIP: If desired, sprinkle cheese with a little oregano or Italian seasoning.

Per sandwich:

CAL	PRO	CARB	FIB	FAT	SAT	CHOL	SOD
428	31g	50g	2g	13g	5g	53mg	1330mg

TUNA MELTS

BROIL

1 (6 1/2-ounce) can water packed tuna, drained
2 tablespoons finely chopped onion
1 to 2 cooked egg whites
1/4 cup reduced calorie mayonnaise
6 English muffin halves
1 1/2 ounces reduced fat Cheddar cheese, shredded

Combine first 4 ingredients. Evenly divide mixture on muffins. Sprinkle with cheese. Place under broiler and cook until heated through and cheese melts. If cheese tends to melt before tuna is heated through, next time add cheese last couple minutes of cooking time. Makes 6 sandwiches.

Per sandwich:

CAL	PRO	CARB	FIB	FAT	SAT	CHOL	SOD
167	14g	14g	<1g	5g	2g	13mg	437mg

GROUND TURKEY SANDWICH

TOP OF STOVE

Great for kids.

3/4 pound ground lean turkey
1 cup finely chopped onion
1 1/2 cups catsup
2 tablespoons white vinegar
2 teaspoons sugar
2 teaspoons dry mustard

Cook ground turkey and onion in medium non-stick skillet until turkey is cooked through and onion is soft. Stir in remaining ingredients. Bring to a boil; reduce heat and simmer, covered, for 20 minutes. Remove cover; continue to cook until most of the liquid mixture has been reduced. Serve on heated hamburger buns, toasted bread or English muffins, if desired. Makes 6 sandwiches.

Per sandwich (filling only):

CAL	PRO	CARB	FIB	FAT	SAT	CHOL	SOD
143	10g	22g	1g	3g	na	na	na

SUBMARINE SANDWICH

Per sandwich:

1 (6-inch) French roll or Hoagie roll
4 thin slices deli turkey
2 teaspoons Dijon mustard
1 slice reduced fat Swiss cheese, cut diagonally into 2 pieces
3 thin tomato slices
1/2 cup shredded lettuce

Cut rolls in half lengthwise; lightly toast. Spread with mustard. Layer with folded turkey slices. Top with cheese slices, tomato and shredded lettuce. Top with remaining bread half. Makes 1 sandwich.

TIP: If you want a hot sandwich, after adding cheese, wrap sandwich in foil. Bake at 350° for about 10 minutes or until heated through. Add remaining ingredients.

Per sandwich:

CAL	PRO	CARB	FIB	FAT	SAT	CHOL	SOD
422	35g	52g	2g	7g	3g	69mg	718mg

BARBECUE CHICKEN PIZZA

OVEN 425°

If you haven't tried barbecue sauce on a pizza, you are in for a treat.

1 chicken breast half, skinned and boned
1 (12-inch) pizza crust
1/3 to 1/2 cup barbecue sauce
1 cup (4-ounces) Lite Mozzarella cheese, shredded
1/4 cup sliced green onion (green part)
1/4 of a medium green pepper, cut into narrow strips

Cut chicken into 1-inch pieces. Place in medium non-stick skillet sprayed with vegetable cooking spray. Cook, stirring frequently, until cooked through. Spread sauce on pizza crust. Sprinkle with cheese, chicken and onion, in that order. Arrange pepper strips over top. Bake at 425° for 10 to 15 minutes, depending on the type of crust used. Makes 8 slices.

Per slice:

CAL	PRO	CARB	FIB	FAT	SAT	CHOL	SOD
130	8g	18g	<1g	2g	1g	4mg	326mg

CANADIAN BACON BREAD SHELL

OVEN 425°

1 Italian Bread Shell, purchased or make you own, see page 35
1/2 cup pizza sauce
1/4 teaspoon basil
3 ounces Lite Mozzarella cheese, shredded
2 ounces very thinly sliced Canadian bacon
2 plum tomatoes, cut into 1/2-inch slices

Place shell on pizza pan. Spread with sauce. Sprinkle with basil and cheese. Arrange Canadian bacon and tomato on top. Bake at 425° for 10 to 12 minutes or until heated through and cheese is melted. Makes 8 slices.

Per slice:

CAL	PRO	CARB	FIB	FAT	SAT	CHOL	SOD
212	13g	33g	1g	3g	1g	8mg	363mg

Cook's Tip

To help prevent pizza crust from gettting soggy, sprinkle a small amount of shredded cheese on crust. Too much sauce and letting the pizza stand before baking can also contribute to a soggy crust.

CANADIAN BACON PINEAPPLE PIZZA

OVEN 450°

1 (10-ounce) can refrigerated pizza crust
1 (8-ounce) can crushed pineapple, drained well
1 to 1$^{1}/_{4}$ cups pizza sauce
6 ounces Lite Mozzarella cheese, shredded
4 ounces Canadian bacon, thinly sliced
$^{1}/_{2}$ small green pepper, cut into narrow strips

Carefully unroll pizza crust; spread evenly in 16-inch pizza pan. Spread pizza sauce over dough. Sprinkle with shredded cheese. Top with Canadian bacon and green pepper. Bake at 450°, on lower shelf of oven, for 12 to 15 minutes, or until pizza is heated through and crust is brown. Makes 12 slices.

Per slice:

CAL	PRO	CARB	FIB	FAT	SAT	CHOL	SOD
126	9g	15g	<1g	3g	1g	9mg	384mg

CHEESEBURGER PIZZA

OVEN 425°

Simple, but good.

$^{1}/_{2}$ pound extra lean ground beef
$^{1}/_{2}$ cup chopped onion
4 ounces fresh mushrooms, sliced
1 (10-ounce) can refrigerated pizza crust
1 cup pizza sauce
1 cup (4-ounces) reduced fat Cheddar cheese, shredded

In medium skillet, cook ground beef, onion and mushrooms until meat is cooked through. Place in colander to drain off fat. Press dough into 10 x 15-inch pan sprayed with vegetable cooking spray. Spread pizza sauce evenly over crust. Top with meat mixture. Sprinkle with cheese. Bake at 425° for 15 to 20 minutes or until lightly browned. Makes 8 servings.

TIP: If desired, substitute ground turkey for the ground beef.

Per serving:

CAL	PRO	CARB	FIB	FAT	SAT	CHOL	SOD
197	14g	20g	<1	7g	3g	29mg	412mg

FRENCH BREAD PIZZA

OVEN 425°

Very good served as a meal with a tossed green salad or as an evening snack (as long as your fat budget will allow it).

1 loaf French bread (about a 1 pound loaf)
1 cup pizza sauce
6 ounces ground turkey sausage
2 tablespoons sliced ripe olives
1/2 of medium green pepper, cut into narrow strips
1 cup (4-ounces) Lite Mozzarella cheese shredded

Brown sausage in non-stick skillet; drain. Cut bread in half lengthwise. Place on baking sheet. Spread with pizza sauce. Arrange sausage over sauce. Top with olives and pepper strips. Sprinkle with cheese. Bake at 425° for 8 to 10 minutes or until heated through and cheese is melted. Makes 6 servings.

TIP: Depending on the length and width of the bread, you may need to use a little more pizza sauce.

Per serving:

CAL	PRO	CARB	FIB	FAT	SAT	CHOL	SOD
343	19g	48g	1g	8g	3g	30mg	857mg

PIZZA QUICK

OVEN 400°

Per serving:

1 (8-inch) flour tortilla
2 tablespoons pizza sauce
2 tablespoons (1/2-ounce) Jarlsberg cheese, shredded
2 tablespoons finely chopped tomato
2 teaspoons chopped green chilies
1 tablespoon finely chopped onion

Place tortilla on baking sheet, bake at 400° for 4 to 5 minutes or until lightly toasted. Remove baking sheet from oven; turn tortilla over. Increase heat to 450°. Spread with sauce, then cheese, tomato, green chilies and onion. Bake at 450° for 10 to 12 minutes or until lightly browned and cheese has melted. Makes 1 serving.

Per serving:

CAL	PRO	CARB	FIB	FAT	SAT	CHOL	SOD
185	7g	25g	2g	7g	na	9mg	323mg

With Lite Mozzarella cheese:

CAL	PRO	CARB	FIB	FAT	SAT	CHOL	SOD
165	8g	25g	2g	3g	1g	5mg	327mg

TORTILLA PIZZA

OVEN 400°

Lower in fat, but high in flavor.

1 10-inch flour tortilla
1/3 cup pizza sauce
2/3 cup (2 1/2-ounces) shredded Lite Mozzarella cheese
2 thin slices Canadian bacon, cut into narrow strips
1/3 cup pineapple tidbits, drained

Place tortilla on baking sheet. Bake at 400° for about 4 minutes. Remove from oven; turn over. Increase oven temperature to 425°. Spread tortilla with sauce. Top with Mozzarella, bacon and pineapple. Bake at 425° for 8 to 10 minutes or until lightly browned. Makes one 10-inch pizza.

Per 1/2 of 10-inch pizza:

CAL	PRO	CARB	FIB	FAT	SAT	CHOL	SOD
265	20g	29g	1g	8g	4g	24mg	856mg

Cook's Tip

Children, in the first two years of life, should not be on a low-fat diet. Beyond age two, keep your child's health in mind, by serving low-fat meats trimmed of skin and fat, more fish in the diet, healthy oils and margarines and low or non-fat dairy products. If there is a history of early heart attacks or high cholesterol levels in the family, testing for cholesterol in children is advisable. Most of all, no matter your child's age, limit their intake of prepared food and "junk" food.

TOMATO CHEESE PIZZA

OVEN 425°

1 can refrigerated pizza crust
1 (16-ounce) can tomatoes, drained, cut into smaller pieces
2 tablespoons finely chopped onion
1/2 teaspoon oregano
1 tablespoon grated Parmesan cheese
1 cup (4-ounce) Lite Mozzarella cheese, shredded

Spread pizza crust in 10 x 15-inch pan. Drain tomatoes thoroughly; cut into small pieces. Combine tomatoes, onion, oregano and Parmesan. Spread on crust. Sprinkle with cheese. Bake at 425° for 10 to 12 minutes or until lightly browned. Makes 8 servings.

Per serving:

CAL	PRO	CARB	FIB	FAT	SAT	CHOL	SOD
134	8g	19g	<1g	2g	1g	5mg	328mg

PEPPER PIZZA

OVEN 425°

A light meatless pizza without extra calories and fat. Serve with a large tossed salad chocked full of healthful goodies.

1 (10-ounce) can refrigerated pizza crust
2 cups (8-ounces) Lite Mozzarella cheese, shredded
1/2 teaspoon Italian seasoning
2/3 cup green pepper, cut into short narrow strips
2/3 cup red pepper, cut into short narrow strips
1/4 cup sliced black olives

On large pizza pan spread pizza dough into a 14-inch circle. Sprinkle with 1 cup of the cheese. Sprinkle with Italian seasoning. Top with peppers and olives. Sprinkle with remaining cheese. Bake at 425° for 12 to 15 minutes or until cheese is melted and crust is golden. Serve immediately. Makes 8 slices.

TIP: A 14-inch circle makes a nice thin crisp crust, especially if you use one of those wonderful pizza pans with tiny holes in the bottom.

Per slice:

CAL	PRO	CARB	FIB	FAT	SAT	CHOL	SOD
168	12g	19g	<1g	4g	2g	8mg	405mg

SAUSAGE PIZZA

TOP OF STOVE
OVEN 425°

Instead of eating pizza as the main (or only) course, why not use it as an accompaniment to a large tossed green salad filled with a variety of fresh vegetables.

1 (16-ounce) package frozen turkey Italian sausage, thawed
1 can refrigerated pizza crust
1 cup (4-ounces) Fontina cheese, shredded
3/4 cup thin sliced onion, separated into rings
1/4 medium green pepper, cut into narrow strips

Shape turkey sausage into small balls. (This is easier to do if you spray your hands lightly with vegetable cooking spray.) Brown in large non-stick skillet until cooked through. Drain. While sausage is cooking, carefully unroll pizza dough. Spread in 10x15-inch pan sprayed with vegetable cooking spray. Prebake in 425° oven for 7 minutes or until dough just begins to turn color. Remove from oven and spread with pizza sauce. Sprinkle cheese over sauce. Arrange sausage over pizza. Cut onion rings into smaller pieces and arrange among the sausage. Add green pepper strips. Bake 10 to 12 minutes or until golden and cheese is bubbly. Makes 8 servings.

Per serving:

CAL	PRO	CARB	FIB	FAT	SAT	CHOL	SOD
249	14g	19g	<1g	12g	5g	51mg	570mg

Meats & Seafood

TERIYAKI BEEF TENDERLOINS

MARINATE
BROIL

By keeping servings small, we can still enjoy an occasional steak.

4 (1-inch) beef tenderloins, about 4 ounces each
1/4 cup plus 2 tablespoons firmly packed light brown sugar
1/4 cup plus 2 tablespoons reduced sodium soy sauce
2 tablespoons white vinegar
1 tablespoon Worcestershire sauce, plus 1 1/2 teaspoons
2 to 3 thin slices fresh ginger

Trim beef of all fat. Combine remaining ingredients; stir to dissolve the sugar. Place steaks in small container or baking dish. Pour marinade over. Cover and refrigerater no longer than 2 hours to blend flavors; turn meat occasionally. When ready to cook, place steaks on broiler pan, 3 to 4 inches from heat. Broil, 3 to 5 minutes on each side for medium rare or until cooked as desired, basting with the marinade.

TIP: For easier cleaning, line pan with foil.

Per 3 ounce serving:

CAL	PRO	CARB	FIB	FAT	SAT	CHOL	SOD
229	26g	7g	0g	9g	3g	65mg	298mg

BEEF TENDERLOINS

TOP OF STOVE

A delightful meat dish made in about 15 minutes.

2 (8-ounce) beef tenderloins, 1-inch thick
Salt and pepper
1 medium onion, sliced and separated into rings
5 tablespoons Sauterne

Cut each tenderloin into two 1/2-inch slices, making 4 tenderloins. Trim off excess fat. Heat medium non-stick skillet sprayed with vegetable cooking spray. Add tenderloin slices. Cook over medium heat, about 3 to 4 minutes on each side, turning once until medium rare or as desired. Sprinkle with salt and pepper. Remove and keep warm. Add onions and Sauterne to skillet. Cook, covered, until onion is just crisp tender, stirring occasionally. Add salt and pepper to taste. Top each tenderloin with onions. Makes 4 servings.

Per serving:

CAL	PRO	CARB	FIB	FAT	SAT	CHOL	SOD
198	27g	4g	<1g	9g	3g	65mg	191mg

Barbecue Flank Steak

Marinate
Broil or Grill

1 (1 to 1¼ pound) flank steak
1 cup thick and rich barbecue sauce (I used Hunt's)
¼ cup reduced sodium soy sauce
2 tablespoons chopped onion
1 large garlic clove, minced
2 thin slices fresh ginger, coarsely chopped

Trim all fat. Place steak in 11 x 7-inch shallow baking dish. Combine remaining ingredients. Pour sauce over top. Turn steak to coat. Cover and marinate in refrigerator several hours or overnight. When ready to serve, place steak on broiler pan and broil, 3 to 4 inches from heat, for 4 to 5 minutes per side for medium rare, basting occasionally with the sauce. If cooking on a grill, place directly on grill, but do not baste with sauce until last 3 or 4 minutes of cooking time. Cut diagonally into thin slices and serve. Makes 4 servings.

TIP: Cooking time may vary according to thickness of steak.

Per 3 ounce serving:

Cal	Pro	Carb	Fib	Fat	Sat	Chol	Sod
275	24g	9g	<1g	10g	4g	57mg	1060mg

Easy One Pan Round Steak

Top of Stove

2 pounds top round steak, about 1-inch thick
3 teaspoons dry mustard
¾ teaspoon salt
¼ teaspoon pepper
1 tablespoon Worcestershire sauce

Trim all fat from meat. Combine mustard, salt and pepper. Rub over meat. Heat large heavy skillet or Dutch oven sprayed with vegetable cooking spray. Brown meat on both sides. Combine Worcestershire sauce with ¾ cup water. Pour over meat. Cover; simmer over low heat, about 1¼ to 1½ hours or until tender. Slice beef diagonally into ½-inch slices. Makes 6 servings.

TIP: Round steak, which has a tendency to be somewhat dry, is enhanced by a nice low-fat gravy. Increase water in recipe to at least 2 cups and Worcestershire sauce to 1½ tablespoons. Follow directions on page 99, to make gravy.

Per serving:

Cal	Pro	Carb	Fib	Fat	Sat	Chol	Sod
206	36g	na	na	6g	2g	95mg	358mg

ROUND STEAK POT ROAST

TOP OF STOVE
OVEN 350°

1 pound top round steak, trimmed of all fat
Salt and pepper
Flour, about 1/4 cup
8 small potatoes
8 small carrots

Sprinkle round steak with salt and pepper. Coat with flour. Heat non-stick skillet sprayed lightly with vegetable cooking spray. Brown meat on both sides. Remove to a Dutch oven or deep oven-going skillet with lid. Add water to almost cover. Bake, covered, at 350° for 1 1/2 to 2 hours, depending on thickness of meat, adding vegetables during last hour of cooking time. Meat should be very tender. Makes 4 servings.

To make gravy: Remove meat and vegetables and keep warm. Bring liquid to a boil. Whisk in a mixture of about 1/3 cup water and 2 tablespoons flour. Cook, stirring frequently, until thickened. If gravy is too thin add a little more flour-water mixture. If too thick, stir in a small amount of water or broth. Add salt and pepper to taste.

Per meat and vegetable serving only:

CAL	PRO	CARB	FIB	FAT	SAT	CHOL	SOD
487	35g	66g	8g	9g	3g	89mg	403mg

EYE OF ROUND BEEF ROAST

OVEN 325°

Sliced thin, this makes a wonderful roast dinner. Use leftovers to make French dip sandwiches.

1 (2 to 2 1/2 pound) eye of round beef roast
1 tablespoon Dijon mustard
Lemon pepper or coarsely ground black pepper

Pat roast dry with paper towels. Place on rack in roasting pan. Spread mustard evenly over surface. Sprinkle with lemon pepper. Bake at 325° for about 1 hour or until a thermometer reaches 140° for medium rare. Remove from oven; cover with foil and let stand 15 to 20 minutes. Slice crosswise into very thin slices. Makes 10 to 12 servings.

TIP: Do not overcook roast or it will be dry and tough. If you enjoy beef cooked medium, you will enjoy this roast cooked medium rare.

Per 3 ounce serving:

CAL	PRO	CARB	FIB	FAT	SAT	CHOL	SOD
143	25g	0g	0g	4g	2g	59mg	53mg

BEEF TENDERLOIN ROAST

OVEN 425°

Delicious served with Bordelaise Sauce, page 180, and Sautéed Vegetables, page 208.

1 ($2^1/_4$-pound) beef tenderloin
1 teaspoon olive oil
Freshly ground black pepper

Trim tenderloin of all fat. Place on rack in roasting pan. Brush with oil and a light sprinkle of pepper. Bake at 425° for 30 to 35 minutes or until meat thermometer reads 140° for medium rare or 150° for medium, or to desired doneness. Remove from oven. Cover tightly with foil; let stand 15 minutes. Makes about eight 3-ounce servings.

Per 3 ounce serving:

CAL	PRO	CARB	FIB	FAT	SAT	CHOL	SOD
184	24g	na	na	9g	3g	71mg	54mg

RUMP POT ROAST

TOP OF STOVE
OVEN 350°

1 ($2^1/_2$-3 pound) rump roast
Salt and pepper
4 medium potatoes, peeled
8 carrots, peeled and cut in half crosswise
1 rutabaga, peeled and cut into 4 wedges
$^1/_4$ cup flour

Spray large pot or Dutch oven with vegetable cooking spray. Heat pan; add roast and quickly brown on all sides. Sprinkle with salt and pepper. Add 3 cups water and heat to boiling. Cover and place in 350° oven. Cook $1^1/_2$ to 2 hours or until almost tender. Add potatoes, carrots and rutabaga. Continue cooking until vegetables are cooked through and meat is tender. Makes four 3-ounce servings with leftovers.

TIP: If vegetables cook before meat is tender, remove and keep warm. The best way to test this roast, is by slicing. If it is easy to slice, it should be tender.

Per 3 ounce serving:

CAL	PRO	CARB	FIB	FAT	SAT	CHOL	SOD
395	32g	53g	8g	6g	2g	82mg	427mg

MARINATED BEEF FOR FAJITAS

MARINATE
TOP OF STOVE

Can be made ahead and reheated.

1 pound flank or skirt steak
3 tablespoons lime juice
1/2 teaspoon ground cumin
1 teaspoon chili powder
1/4 teaspoon garlic powder

Trim fat from meat; place in shallow dish. Combine remaining ingredients; pour over meat. Turn to coat. Cover; refrigerate 2 to 3 hours to marinate. When ready to cook; remove from marinade. Slice, across the grain into 1/8-inch slices. Cook about 1/4 of meat at a time, in non-stick skillet sprayed with vegetable cooking spray. Heat should be fairly high to cook meat quickly. Makes 4 meat servings (about 3 fajitas per person).

TIP: Serve with warm flour tortillas, sautéed peppers and onions, salsa (drained) and lite sour cream. Let everyone make their own.

Per meat serving:

CAL	PRO	CARB	FIB	FAT	SAT	CHOL	SOD
182	23g	2g	<1g	9g	4g	57mg	77mg

PEPPER STEAK

MARINATE
TOP OF STOVE

Delicious served over rice.

1 pound top round steak
1 teaspoon cornstarch
2 tablespoons reduced sodium soy sauce
1 tablespoon sugar
2 medium green peppers, cut into narrow strips
2 large tomatoes, coarsely chopped

Cut steak crosswise into narrow strips about 1/8-inch thick. Combine cornstarch, soy sauce and sugar. Pour over steak; marinate in refrigerator 2 to 3 hours or overnight. When ready to serve, quickly brown steak in non-stick skillet sprayed with vegetable cooking spray. (Do not overcook or meat will be tough.) Remove meat. Add green pepper; sauté until just crisp tender. If peppers stick to pan, add a small amount of water. Add tomatoes and beef; cook until heated through. Makes 4 servings.

Per serving:

CAL	PRO	CARB	FIB	FAT	SAT	CHOL	SOD
216	26g	10g	2g	5g	2g	59mg	302mg

Mushroom Round Steak

Oven 325°

1 pound top round steak
1 (4-ounce) can mushroom stems and pieces
1 medium onion, sliced and separated into rings
1 (14½-ounce) can regular strength beef broth
Salt and pepper to taste
2 tablespoons cornstarch

Cut meat into 4 serving size pieces. Place in Dutch oven. Add mushrooms, onion, broth and salt and pepper. Cover; bake at 325° for 2½ to 3 hours or until tender. Remove meat and keep warm. Combine cornstarch with about ½ cup water. Stir into broth mixture. Place on burner; cook over medium heat until thickened. Taste for seasoning, adding more salt and pepper if needed. Makes 4 servings.

TIP: Round steak must be cooked until very tender or it will be tough. Prime rib it is not, but a good gravy will enhance the flavor. See page 99.

Per serving:

Cal	Pro	Carb	Fib	Fat	Sat	Chol	Sod
195	27g	9g	1g	5g	2g	59mg	480mg

Ground Beef Noodle Dish

Top of Stove

Great on those rush days.

¾ pound extra lean ground beef
1 medium onion, sliced and separated into rings
1 (14½-ounce) can Italian stewed tomatoes, with juice
¼ teaspoon salt
⅛ teaspoon pepper
1 cup cooked wide noodles

Brown ground beef and onion in large skillet; pour off drippings. Add tomatoes (cut into smaller pieces), salt and pepper. Bring to a boil, reduce heat and simmer 10 minutes. Add noodles and cook a couple of minutes or until noodles are heated through. Makes 4 servings.

Per serving:

Cal	Pro	Carb	Fib	Fat	Sat	Chol	Sod
241	20g	25g	2g	7g	3g	53mg	401mg

BEEF BARLEY STOVE TOP DINNER

TOP OF STOVE

A nice blend of flavors. Makes 6 generous servings. Best served same day made.

1 pound extra lean ground beef
1 cup chopped onion
1 (14.5-ounce) can chunky stewed tomatoes, with juice
3/4 cup uncooked barley
1 (10-ounce) package frozen mixed vegetables
Salt and pepper to taste

Cook ground beef and onion in large skillet or pot, until beef is browned. Pour into colander to drain off fat. Return to skillet. Stir in tomatoes and barley. Add 3 cups water. Bring to a boil; reduce heat and simmer, covered, for 30 minutes. Add vegetables; cover and simmer about 30 minutes or until vegetables are cooked through and barley is tender. If desired, add salt and pepper to taste. Makes 6 servings.

Per serving:

CAL	PRO	CARB	FIB	FAT	SAT	CHOL	SOD
246	19g	30g	8g	7g	3g	48mg	241mg

BEEF AND POTATOES

TOP OF STOVE
OVEN 450°

A good family stand-by.

4 small baking potatoes
1 pound extra lean ground beef
1 1/4 cups thick n' chunky salsa
1/3 cup sliced ripe olives (optional)
1/2 cup (2 ounces) reduced fat Cheddar cheese, shredded

Wrap each potato in foil. Bake at 450° for 45 to 60 minutes or until potatoes are cooked through. About 15 minutes before potatoes are done, brown ground beef in medium skillet. Place in colander to drain off fat. Return to skillet; stir in salsa (and olives if using). Bring to a boil; reduce heat and simmer until liquid is absorbed. On each serving plate, cut a potato into quarters and arrange spoke fashion. Spoon 1/4 of meat mixture in center of potato. Sprinkle with 1/4 of the cheese. Makes 4 servings.

Per serving (without olives):

CAL	PRO	CARB	FIB	FAT	SAT	CHOL	SOD
426	30g	49g	5g	13g	7g	80mg	254mg

Applesauce Meat Loaf

Oven 350°

Applesauce adds flavor and moisture to make a tasty meat loaf.

1 pound extra lean ground beef
1/2 cup fresh bread crumbs
1/2 cup applesauce
2 egg whites
3/4 teaspoon salt
1/4 teaspoon freshly ground black pepper

In medium mixing bowl, gently combine ingredients until well mixed. Place in shallow baking dish; shape into about a 7-inch round loaf. Bake at 350° for 50 to 60 minutes or until cooked through. Remove meat loaf from pan immediately to prevent soaking up excess fat from drippings. Makes 4 servings.

Per serving:

Cal	Pro	Carb	Fib	Fat	Sat	Chol	Sod
206	24g	6g	<1g	9g	4g	70mg	523mg

Meat Loaf

Oven 350°

1 1/2 pounds extra lean ground beef
1/2 cup finely chopped green pepper
1/2 cup finely chopped onion
1 teaspoon salt
1 tablespoon prepared mustard
1/4 cup chili sauce

In medium mixing bowl, gently combine ingredients until well mixed. Place in shallow baking dish; shape into about a 7-inch round. Bake at 350° for 50 to 60 minutes or until cooked through. Remove meat loaf from baking dish immediately to prevent meat from soaking up drippings. Makes 4 servings.

Per serving (about 4 1/2 ounces):

Cal	Pro	Carb	Fib	Fat	Sat	Chol	Sod
289	34g	8g	<1g	14g	6g	105mg	911mg

Cook's Tip

To remove as much fat as possible from cooked ground beef, pour meat into colander; let stand a few minutes to drain off fat.

GROUND BEEF FAJITAS

TOP OF STOVE

A twist to the popular beef fajitas.

1 pound extra lean ground beef
3/4 of a medium green pepper, cut into narrow strips
1 small onion, thinly sliced, separated into rings
1 cup well-drained salsa
1/3 cup Lite sour cream
8 (8-inch) flour tortillas, warmed

In large skillet, combine ground beef, pepper and onion. Cook until beef is lightly browned and cooked through. Pour into colander to drain off fat. Divide mixture evenly on tortillas. Top each with 2 tablespoons salsa and 2 teaspoons sour cream. Roll tortilla around filling. Makes 8 fajitas.

Per fajita:

CAL	PRO	CARB	FIB	FAT	SAT	CHOL	SOD
222	15g	24g	2g	9g	4g	39mg	202mg

EASY GROUND BEEF TACOS

TOP OF STOVE

Try a taco buffet and let everyone make their own.

1 pound extra lean ground beef
1 1/4 cups salsa
10 packaged cooked taco shells, heated
1 cup (4-ounces) reduced fat Cheddar cheese, shredded
2 cups shredded lettuce
1/2 cup chopped tomatoes

Brown ground beef in medium skillet. Pour in colander to drain off all fat. Return to skillet. Stir in salsa. Bring to a boil; reduce heat and simmer until liquid is absorbed. Spoon some of the meat mixture into each taco shell. Top each with some of the cheese, lettuce and tomatoes. Makes 10 tacos.

Per taco:

CAL	PRO	CARB	FIB	FAT	SAT	CHOL	SOD
172	13g	12g	2g	9g	3g	36mg	202mg

QUICK VEAL SCALLOPINI

TOP OF STOVE

1 pound thinly sliced veal scallopini
Lemon pepper
Paprika
2 tablespoons lemon juice
1/4 cup water
Parsley

Cut scallopini into 4 serving size pieces. Sprinkle lightly with lemon pepper and paprika. Place in heated non-stick skillet sprayed with vegetable cooking spray. Quickly cook, 1 to 2 minutes on each side, or until browned and tender. Don't overcook or veal will be tough. Remove and keep warm. Add lemon juice and water to skillet. Cook, until heated through, stirring in any brown bits in the pan. Spoon over veal; sprinkle with parsley. Make 4 servings.

Per serving:

CAL	PRO	CARB	FIB	FAT	SAT	CHOL	SOD
243	26g	<1g	<1g	15g	6g	100mg	67mg

Cook's Tip

Raw meat is difficult to cut into thin slices. To make slicing easier, place meat in freezer for about 30 minutes or until firm to the touch, but not frozen. Slice meat across the grain into thin slices.

~

Tender cuts of meat, such as beef tenderloin, should never be marinated longer than 2 hours. Less tender cuts can be marinated several hours or overnight.

BAKED PORK CHOPS WITH RICE

OVEN 350°

This main dish can be put together in less than 5 minutes.

4 rib-cut pork chops, cut 1-inch thick
Salt and pepper
4 onion slices
6 tablespoons uncooked long-grain rice
1 (14.5-ounce) can stewed tomatoes, with juice
Dried basil

Lightly spray an 8 x 8-inch baking dish with vegetable cooking spray. Sprinkle pork chops with salt and pepper; place in baking dish. Top each pork chop with an onion slice. Evenly sprinkle raw rice around pork chops. Pour tomatoes over top (cut up larger pieces of tomato). Sprinkle lightly with basil. Cover tightly and bake at 350° for 1½ hours or until meat is tender. Makes 4 servings.

Per serving:

CAL	PRO	CARB	FIB	FAT	SAT	CHOL	SOD
350	31g	24g	2g	14g	5g	78mg	263mg

COMPANY PORK CHOPS

TOP OF STOVE
OVEN 350°

A great company recipe. Serve when you feel you can afford to splurge on your fat and cholesterol allowance.

4 loin-cut pork chops, cut 1-inch thick
4 onion slices, ½-inch thick
Cracked pepper
1 chicken bouillon cube, crushed
2 teaspoons prepared mustard
4 (canned) crab apples

Trim fat from pork chops. Place in non-stick skillet sprayed with vegetable cooking spray; cook until just lightly browned on both sides. Place onion slices in 8 x 8-inch baking dish. Top with pork chops. Sprinkle lightly with cracked pepper. Combine bouillon and mustard with ¼ cup hot water. Pour over pork chops. Cover with foil; bake at 350° for 40 to 45 minutes or until tender. Serve each pork chop garnished with a crab apple. Makes 4 servings.

Per serving:

CAL	PRO	CARB	FIB	FAT	SAT	CHOL	SOD
304	34g	7g	<1g	15g	5g	104mg	388mg

GRILLED PORK CHOPS DIJON

GRILL

4 loin-cut pork chops, cut 1/2-inch thick
3 tablespoons Dijon mustard
1/4 teaspoon dried tarragon
1/4 teaspoon garlic powder
Cracked pepper

Trim pork chops of all fat. Place on heated grill sprayed with vegetable cooking spray. Cook about 14 minutes. Turn; cook about 8 minutes. Combine mustard, tarragon and garlic powder. Brush top of each pork chop with some of the sauce. Cook about 2 to 3 minutes or until cooked through. Sprinkle lightly with a little cracked pepper. Makes 4 servings.

Per serving:

CAL	PRO	CARB	FIB	FAT	SAT	CHOL	SOD
145	17g	1g	0g	8g	3g	52mg	184mg

PORK CHOPS 'N GRAVY

TOP OF STOVE

You don't have to give up gravy completely. This is a very good lower fat version.

4 loin-cut pork chops, cut 1/2-inch thick
Salt and pepper
1/4 teaspoon Herbs of Province
1/2 cup nonfat milk
2 tablespoons flour

Trim fat from pork chops. Quickly brown on both sides, in large non-stick skillet sprayed with vegetable cooking spray. Sprinkle with salt, pepper and Herbs of Province. Add 1/2 cup water; cover and simmer about 20 minutes or until pork chops are tender and cooked through. Remove from skillet and keep warm. Place milk and then flour in a small jar. Cover and shake to blend. Gradually add to hot drippings in skillet. Cook until thickened, stirring frequently. If desired, add additional salt and pepper (or other seasonings) to taste. Makes 4 servings.

Per serving:

CAL	PRO	CARB	FIB	FAT	SAT	CHOL	SOD
203	23g	5g	<1g	10g	3g	69mg	118mg

PORK CHOP CASSEROLE

TOP OF STOVE
OVEN 350°

An easy dinner meal.

8 rib-cut pork chops, cut 1/2-inch thick
1 cup chopped onion
2 cups chopped Rome apples
1/4 cup raisins
2 cups seasoned herb stuffing mix
1 teaspoon salt

Quickly brown pork chops in non-stick skillet sprayed with vegetable cooking spray. Remove and set aside. Add onion to skillet; cook until crisp tender. Stir in apple, raisins, stuffing mix and salt. Arrange 4 pork chops in 2-quart shallow baking dish. Top with half the stuffing. Cover with remaining pork chops; top with stuffing. Add 2 tablespoons water. Cover; bake at 350° for 45 to 50 minutes or until pork chops are tender. (I like to remove cover last 10 minutes of cooking time.) Makes 8 servings.

TIP: These servings are small.

Per serving:

CAL	PRO	CARB	FIB	FAT	SAT	CHOL	SOD
343	24g	23g	2g	17g	5g	67mg	630mg

PORK CHOPS WITH PECAN SAUCE

TOP OF STOVE

Pecans can be quickly toasted in microwave, if desired.

4 loin-cut pork chops, cut 1-inch thick
2 tablespoons coarsely chopped pecans, toasted
1/4 cup orange juice
3 tablespoons orange marmalade
1 green onion, cut diagonally into 1-inch slices

Trim all excess fat from chops. Cook in non-stick skillet sprayed with vegetable cooking spray, cooking 6 to 8 minutes per side or until cooked through. Meanwhile, in small sauce pan, combine pecans, juice and marmalade. Bring to a boil, reduce heat and simmer 3 to 4 minutes. Add onion and simmer 1 minute. Serve each pork chop topped with 1/4 of the sauce. Makes 4 servings.

Per serving:

CAL	PRO	CARB	FIB	FAT	SAT	CHOL	SOD
341	33g	13g	<1g	17g	5g	104mg	78mg

PORK FRIED RICE

TOP OF STOVE

I prefer to use an egg in this recipe rather than a substitute.

1 cup uncooked rice, cooked and chilled
1/2 cup chopped onion
6 ounces pork tenderloin
1/4 cup reduced sodium soy sauce
1 egg, lightly beaten
2 green onions, sliced (1/4 cup)

Spray large non-stick skillet with vegetable cooking spray. Add onions and cook until soft, stirring frequently. Remove onions; spray skillet again. Cut tenderloin across the grain into 1/8-inch thick slices. Cut each slice in half. Cook, over medium-high heat, stirring constantly, until lightly browned and just cooked through. Return onion to skillet. Stir in chilled rice and soy sauce. Push rice mixture to the sides, making a well in center of skillet. Add egg to middle. Cook until egg is done, stirring to scramble. Stir egg into rice along with the green onion. Cook until heated through. Makes 6 servings.

Variation: Use chicken, ham or beef.

Per serving:

CAL	PRO	CARB	FIB	FAT	SAT	CHOL	SOD
221	10g	30g	<1g	2g	<1g	56mg	348mg

PORK STIR-FRY

TOP OF STOVE

Very good served over rice.

1/2 pound pork tenderloin
2 medium carrots, sliced thin
4 ounces fresh Chinese pea pods
3/4 cup pineapple juice
2 tablespoons reduced sodium soy sauce
1 tablespoon cornstarch

Cut pork on the bias into thin slices. Cut slices into 1-inch strips. Set aside. Separately, steam carrots and pea pods until just crisp tender. Place pork in heated non-stick skillet sprayed with vegetable cooking spray. Cook, stirring frequently, until lightly browned and no longer pink. Combine pineapple juice and soy sauce. Stir a small amount of the liquid into cornstarch; stir to dissolve. Combine with remaining liquid. Add to skillet. Cook, stirring frequently until thickened. Stir in carrots and pea pods. Continue to cook to heat through. Makes 4 servings.

Per serving:

CAL	PRO	CARB	FIB	FAT	SAT	CHOL	SOD
159	14g	14g	2g	2g	<1g	40mg	296mg

PORK ROAST DIJON

OVEN 350°

$2^1/2$ pound boneless pork top loin roast
2 teaspoons Dijon mustard
$^1/4$ teaspoon salt
$^1/8$ teaspoon pepper
$^1/4$ teaspoon rosemary

Pat roast dry with a paper towel. Combine remaining ingredients. Spread on roast. Place fat side up, on rack in roasting pan. Roast, uncovered, about $1^1/2$ hours or until thermometer reaches 170°. Remove from oven. Cover with foil; let stand 15 minutes before slicing. Makes ten 3-ounce servings.

Per serving:

CAL	PRO	CARB	FIB	FAT	SAT	CHOL	SOD
152	26g	<1g	<1g	4g	2g	85mg	127mg

PORK TENDERLOIN WITH PINEAPPLE

TOP OF STOVE

A winner when served over hot cooked noodles or rice.

$^3/4$ pound pork tenderloin
$1^1/4$ cups pineapple juice
1 (8-ounce) can pineapple chunks, do not drain
2 small thin slices fresh ginger
2 green onions, sliced diagonally into 1-inch pieces
1 tablespoon cornstarch

Cut pork tenderloin diagonally into $^1/2$-inch slices. Lightly brown on both sides in medium non-stick skillet sprayed with vegetable cooking spray. Add pineapple juice, canned pineapple and ginger. Bring to a boil; reduce heat and add onion. Combine cornstarch with 2 tablespoons water; stir to blend. Add to skillet. Cook, stirring frequently, until thickened. Remove ginger slices. Makes 4 servings.

Per serving:

CAL	PRO	CARB	FIB	FAT	SAT	CHOL	SOD
198	19g	23g	1g	3g	1g	60mg	46mg

HAM WITH MUSTARD GLAZE

OVEN 325°

Always a favorite. Leftovers are nice for sandwiches or casseroles.

1 cooked boneless lean ham (desired size)
1/2 cup firmly packed light brown sugar
1/4 cup orange juice
1/2 teaspoon dry mustard

Place ham on rack in roasting pan, fat side up. Bake at 325° for 20 minutes per pound or until heated through. Meanwhile, combine remaining ingredients. During last 30 minutes of baking time, brush ham generously with some of the glaze. Continue basting every 10 minutes. Remove from oven. Cover with foil and let stand 15 to 20 minutes before slicing.

Per 3 ounce serving:

CAL	PRO	CARB	FIB	FAT	SAT	CHOL	SOD
133	21g	0g	0g	5g	2g	47mg	1128mg

HOT MOSTACCIOLI WITH HAM

TOP OF STOVE
OVEN 350°

A lot of flavor with just a few ingredients. Serve with a nice salad and Focaccia (page 34).

8 ounces uncooked mostaccioli
1 small bunch green onions, about 7 or 8
1 teaspoon Canola oil
4 ounces lean ham, cut into small cubes
2 tablespoons sliced almonds
1/2 cup freshly grated Parmesan cheese, divided

Cook noodles according to package directions. Meanwhile, slice whole onions into 1/2-inch slices. Sauté in heated oil in small non-stick skillet. When onions are slightly soft, stir in ham and almonds. Cook, stirring frequently, until heated through. Toss with hot, drained noodles and all but 1 tablespoon Parmesan. Pour into 1 1/2-quart baking dish sprayed with vegetable cooking spray. Sprinkle the 1 tablespoon cheese over top. Bake at 350° for 10 minutes. Serve immediately while very hot. Makes 4 servings.

TIP: If casserole appears somewhat dry, stir in about 2 tablespoons skim milk just before baking.

Per serving:

CAL	PRO	CARB	FIB	FAT	SAT	CHOL	SOD
402	23g	56g	1g	9g	3g	27mg	644mg

COOKING TIME FOR FISH

Measure all fish at its thickest part. Estimate 10 minutes cooking time per inch. Baking temperature should be 450°. Total cooking time applies to whatever cooking method is used - baking, broiling, grilling, frying, etc. For example, if baking a whole fish and the fish measures 3 inches at its thickest part, you will need to bake for 30 minutes at 450°. If broiling or grilling a steak 1½-inches thick, broil 7½ minutes on each side. If the fish is less than 1-inch thick, there is no need to turn. Test for doneness with a wooden toothpick (if it comes out clean and dry, the fish should be done). It is also done when it flakes easily with a fork.

NOTE: This method works most of the time, but I find when cooking a whole fish, stuffed or unstuffed, I often have to increase the cooking time. This could be due to variations in oven temperatures and the temperature of the fish.

BAKED SALMON STEAKS

OVEN 450°

4 salmon steaks, cut 1-inch thick
2 tablespoons soft tub margarine, melted
½ teaspoon Worcestershire sauce
1 teaspoon fresh lemon juice

Place steaks in shallow baking pan sprayed with vegetable cooking spray. Combine remaining ingredients. Brush steaks with some of the sauce. Bake at 450° for 10 minutes, basting occasionally with the sauce. Start testing for doneness after 8 minutes of cooking time. Fish should flake easily when done. Makes 4 servings.

Per serving:

CAL	PRO	CARB	FIB	FAT	SAT	CHOL	SOD
240	31g	0g	0g	12g	2g	56mg	95mg

BAKED WHOLE SALMON

OVEN 450°

A great Pacific Northwest treat.

Whole salmon, cleaned and wiped dry
Salt and pepper
1 large lemon, sliced
1 medium onion, sliced and separated into rings
6 slices bacon

Sprinkle salmon with salt and pepper (inside and out). Place on large sheet of heavy duty foil in large shallow baking pan. Place 3 bacon slices lengthwise inside salmon. Stuff with lemon and onion slices. Place remaining bacon on top of fish. Wrap foil to seal. Bake at 450° for 10 minutes per inch measuring salmon at its thickest part. (A large salmon may take a little longer.) Test for doneness with a wooden toothpick. If it comes out clean and dry and the salmon flakes easily, it is done. Discard bacon, lemon and onion.

Per 3 ounce serving:

CAL	PRO	CARB	FIB	FAT	SAT	CHOL	SOD
157	23g	0g	0g	6g	1g	42mg	50mg

TERIYAKI SALMON STEAKS

MARINATE
BROIL

Teriyaki seems to be everyone's favorite.

4 salmon steaks, cut 1-inch thick
3 tablespoons Canola oil
2 tablespoons fresh lemon juice
2 tablespoons reduced sodium soy sauce
1/2 teaspoon dry mustard
1/2 teaspoon ground ginger

Place steaks in shallow dish. Combine remaining ingredients; pour over steaks. Cover; marinate in refrigerator for at least 1 hour, turning occasionally. Drain; reserve marinade. Place steaks on rack in broiling pan. Broil for 5 minutes; turn and brush with marinade. Broil steaks for 5 minutes or until tests done. Makes 4 servings.

Per 4-ounce serving:

CAL	PRO	CARB	FIB	FAT	SAT	CHOL	SOD
251	31g	<1g	0g	12g	2g	56mg	163mg

SALMON ROUELLES

BROIL

These are especially attractive for a company meal, yet very quick to prepare.

1 center-cut salmon fillet (1 1/2 pounds), skin removed
Salt and pepper
1 lemon (4 thin slices and 1 tablespoon juice)
2 tablespoons soft tub margarine, melted
1/2 teaspoon Worcestershire sauce
4 small sprigs fresh parsley

Remove any bones you can see from the fillet. Cut cross-wise into 3/4-inch slices. Arrange 2 strips, cut-side up, with the thin ends overlapping the thick, forming a circle. Add a third strip to the center, filling in the circle. Tie dental floss or string around outside of rouelles, making a secure circle without spaces between strips. Carefully place in shallow pan. (At this point, salmon can be covered and chilled until ready to cook.) Sprinkle lightly with salt and pepper. Combine lemon juice, margarine and Worcestershire sauce. Brush rouelles with some of the sauce. Place under broiler and cook about 5 to 6 minutes or until tests done, basting once with the sauce. Cut a slit in each lemon slice, cutting just to the center. Twist; place on rouelles. Garnish with parsley. Makes 4 servings.

Per serving:

CAL	PRO	CARB	FIB	FAT	SAT	CHOL	SOD
345	37g	<1g	0g	20g	4g	118mg	244mg

TARRAGON SALMON

TOP OF STOVE
OVEN 450°

1 1/4 pound salmon fillet
1/2 teaspoon Canola oil
1/4 teaspoon dried tarragon
1 tablespoon Dijon mustard
1/4 cup white wine
1 tablespoon soft tub margarine

Place fillet, skin-side down, on shallow baking pan sprayed with vegetable cooking spray. In small saucepan, combine oil, tarragon, mustard, wine and margarine. Bring to a boil; reduce heat and simmer 2 to 3 minutes. Pour over salmon. Bake at 450° for 10 to 12 minutes depending on thickness of fillet. Cut crosswise into 4 pieces. Makes 4 servings.

Per serving:

CAL	PRO	CARB	FIB	FAT	SAT	CHOL	SOD
253	31g	<1g	0g	12g	2g	56mg	140mg

BAKED CATFISH PARMESAN

OVEN 450°

The Parmesan coating is excellent and can be used on any mild white fish.

1 pound catfish
3 tablespoons nonfat yogurt
1/3 cup freshly grated Parmesan cheese
2 tablespoons flour
1/8 teaspoon pepper
1/4 teaspoon paprika

Wash fish; pat dry. Cut into 4 equal portions. Brush fillets lightly with yogurt. Combine remaining ingredients. Dip fish in Parmesan mixture, turning to coat both sides. Place on shallow baking pan sprayed with vegetable cooking spray. Bake at 450° for 8 to 12 minutes, depending on thickness, until fish flakes easily with a fork. Makes 4 servings.

Per serving:

CAL	PRO	CARB	FIB	FAT	SAT	CHOL	SOD
194	26g	4g	<1g	8g	3g	73mg	255mg

EASY SKILLET FISH DISH

TOP OF STOVE

1 pound orange roughy or turbot fillets
1 teaspoon olive oil
2 medium peppers (1 red and 1 green) cut into narrow strips
1 medium onion, sliced, separated into rings
1/2 teaspoon dried basil
Salt and pepper to taste

Cut fillets into 4 serving pieces. Heat oil in large non-stick skillet. Add peppers and onion. Arrange fillets on top. Sprinkle with seasonings. Cover; cook over low heat for 12 minutes. Uncover; continue cooking until fish flakes easily with a fork and vegetables are crisp tender. Makes 4 servings.

Per serving:

CAL	PRO	CARB	FIB	FAT	SAT	CHOL	SOD
131	19g	9g	2g	2g	<1g	24mg	185mg

FILLETS WITH LEMON PEPPER

BROIL

1 pound ling cod, cut into 4 servings
2 tablespoons soft tub margarine, melted
1½ teaspoons dry mustard
¼ teaspoon lemon pepper (or to taste)

Place fillets in shallow baking pan. Combine remaining ingredients. Brush some of the sauce on the fillets. Place under broiler and cook 5 to 10 minutes, depending on thickness of fish or until fish flakes easily with fork, brushing occasionally with the sauce. Makes 4 servings.

Per serving:

CAL	PRO	CARB	FIB	FAT	SAT	CHOL	SOD
148	20g	<1g	0g	6g	1g	50mg	129mg

FILLET OF SOLE WITH DILL

BROIL

1 pound fillet of sole (4 fillets)
2 tablespoons fresh lime juice
1 small garlic clove, minced
¼ teaspoon dried dill weed
Salt and pepper

Place fillets in shallow baking pan sprayed with vegetable cooking spray. Combine lime juice, garlic and dill weed. Brush some of the sauce on the fillets. Sprinkle lightly with salt and pepper. Place under broiler; cook 8 to 10 minutes, depending on thickness, or until fish flakes easily with fork, brushing occasionally with remaining sauce. Makes 4 servings.

Per serving:

CAL	PRO	CARB	FIB	FAT	SAT	CHOL	SOD
111	22g	1g	0g	1g	<1g	63mg	150mg

LINDA'S FAVORITE HALIBUT

OVEN 450°

1 pound halibut, about 1-inch thick
1/2 teaspoon garlic salt
3 tablespoons Lite sour cream
1 green onion, chopped
2 teaspoons fresh grated Parmesan cheese

Pat halibut dry. Sprinkle with garlic salt. Combine onion and sour cream; spread over fish. Sprinkle Parmesan over top. Bake at 450° for ten minutes or until tests done. Makes 4 servings.

TIP: This recipe is good with most white fish.

Per serving:

CAL	PRO	CARB	FIB	FAT	SAT	CHOL	SOD
126	20g	<1g	<1g	4g	1g	40mg	297mg

HALIBUT WITH TOMATO

OVEN 450°

1 pound halibut, about 1-inch thick
1/4 cup fresh lemon juice
2 plum tomatoes, chopped
2 green onions, sliced on the diagonal
1/4 teaspoon dried basil
1/4 teaspoon salt

Place halibut in baking dish. Pour lemon juice over top. Cover with tomatoes and onion. Sprinkle with basil and salt. Bake at 450° for 10 minutes or until fish flakes easily with fork. Makes 4 servings.

Per serving:

CAL	PRO	CARB	FIB	FAT	SAT	CHOL	SOD
137	24g	3g	<1g	3g	<1g	36mg	198mg

BASIL

Rainbow Trout

Oven 450°

1 pound Rainbow trout
2 tablespoons olive oil
2 tablespoons fresh lemon juice
1/4 teaspoon dried oregano
1/8 teaspoon salt
1/8 teaspoon pepper

Cut trout into 4 serving pieces. Place in 8-inch glass baking dish. Combine remaining ingredients; pour over fish. Cover; marinate in refrigerator for about an hour. Remove from marinade; place in shallow baking dish. Bake at 450°, basting occasionally with the marinade, until fish flakes easily and tests done. Makes 4 servings.

Per serving:

Cal	Pro	Carb	Fib	Fat	Sat	Chol	Sod
170	24g	<1g	0g	7g	1g	67mg	85mg

Red Snapper with Peppers

Broil

1 pound fillet of red snapper
4 teaspoons reduced sodium soy sauce
1/4 teaspoon ground ginger
2 medium peppers, 1 red and 1 green, cut into narrow strips
6 ounces fresh mushrooms, sliced

Place fillet in shallow baking dish. Combine soy sauce and ginger; brush over fish. Place under broiler and cook 8 to 10 minutes, depending on thickness of fish or until fish flakes easily with fork. Meanwhile, in large non-stick skillet sprayed with vegetable cooking spray, cook peppers and mushrooms until just crisp tender. Serve vegetables with or on snapper. Makes 4 servings.

Per serving:

Cal	Pro	Carb	Fib	Fat	Sat	Chol	Sod
159	26g	5g	1g	2g	<1g	43mg	215mg

GRILLED SHRIMP KABOBS

GRILL

Remember, if using wooden skewers, they must be soaked in water for 20 minutes before using.

16 large uncooked shrimp
16 Chinese pea pods, cooked to crisp tender
2 tablespoons soft tub margarine, melted
1½ teaspoons fresh lemon juice
¼ teaspoon dill weed
Dash of pepper

Wrap a pea pod around center of each shrimp; secure with wooden toothpick. Place 4 shrimp on each skewer. Combine remaining ingredients; brush shrimp lightly with some of the sauce. Place on hot grill sprayed with vegetable cooking spray. Cooking time can vary according to the size of the shrimp and how hot the grill is. Shrimp does cook very quickly, so watch for doneness; turn and cook other side, brushing with more of the sauce. Makes 4 servings.

NOTE: Can use cooked shrimp and decrease cooking time.

Per serving:

CAL	PRO	CARB	FIB	FAT	SAT	CHOL	SOD
50	7g	4g	1g	<1g	<1g	56mg	66mg

Cook's Tip

When shopping, always read labels carefully. Many are written to intentionally mislead you into buying their product.

Poultry

CHICKEN FAJITAS

MARINATE
TOP OF STOVE
OVEN 350°

4 chicken breast halves, skinned and boned
2 garlic cloves, chopped fine
1/4 cup fresh lime juice, (1 to 2 limes)
8 (8-inch) flour tortillas
1 cup salsa
1/2 cup Lite sour cream

Cut chicken cross-wise into 1/2-inch strips. In medium size bowl, combine garlic and lime juice. Add chicken and toss to coat. Place in refrigerator and marinate 45 minutes, stirring occasionally. Drain off liquid; cook in non-stick pan sprayed with vegetable cooking spray until lightly browned and cooked through.

Meanwhile, wrap tortillas in foil and heat in 350° oven until warm. To serve, place a portion of chicken on each tortilla, top with 2 tablespoons salsa and 1 tablespoon sour cream. Fold tortilla around filling and enjoy. Makes 4 servings of 2 each.

VARIATION: Another popular way to eat chicken fajitas is with sautéed onions and peppers. See recipe below.

Per serving:

CAL	PRO	CARB	FIB	FAT	SAT	CHOL	SOD
417	35g	44g	3g	13g	4g	85mg	406mg

SAUTÉED ONIONS AND PEPPERS

TOP OF STOVE

Serve with chicken or beef fajitas.

1 tablespoon olive oil
1/4 teaspoon paprika
1/2 red pepper, cut into narrow strips
1/2 green pepper, cut into narrow strips
2 large onions, thinly sliced, separated into rings
Salt and pepper to taste

Heat oil in large skillet. Stir in paprika. Add peppers and onions. Cook over medium heat, stirring frequently, until vegetables are just crisp tender. Makes enough vegetables for 8 fajitas.

Per serving of Onions and Peppers:

CAL	PRO	CARB	FIB	FAT	SAT	CHOL	SOD
50	1g	8g	2g	2g	.3g	0mg	79mg

Oven Baked Chicken

Marinate
Oven 425°

4 chicken breast halves, skinned
1 1/4 cups buttermilk
1 cup flour
1 teaspoon salt
1/2 teaspoon pepper
1 teaspoon paprika

Place chicken, rounded side down, in glass baking dish. Pour buttermilk over top. Marinate in refrigerator at least one hour or more, basting frequently with the buttermilk. When ready to bake, combine remaining ingredients and mix well. Drain chicken pieces slightly and coat with flour mixture. Place, rounded side up, on shallow baking pan sprayed with vegetable cooking spray. Bake at 425° for 15 minutes. Reduce heat to 350° and continue to bake for 15 minutes. Turn chicken and bake 15 minutes. Turn again and bake 15 minutes or until golden and tender. (If there is dry flour remaining on the chicken, brush lightly with a little water or the remaining buttermilk.) Makes 4 servings.

Per serving:

Cal	Pro	Carb	Fib	Fat	Sat	Chol	Sod
286	32g	28g	1g	4g	1g	75mg	677mg

Teriyaki Chicken

Marinate
Oven 350°

4 chicken breast halves, skinned
1/4 cup chopped onion
1 garlic clove, minced
2 tablespoons sugar
1/2 teaspoon dried ginger
1/2 cup reduced sodium soy sauce

Wash chicken and pat dry. Place in a dish just large enough to hold the chicken. Combine remaining ingredients with 1/4 cup water. Pour over chicken. Marinate for one hour, basting chicken with sauce or turning frequently. Place chicken, rounded side down, in shallow roasting pan. Pour sauce over top. Bake at 350° for 30 minutes. Turn chicken and bake 15 to 20 minutes or until cooked through, basting frequently with the sauce. Frequent basting will help to keep the chicken moist. Makes 4 servings.

Per serving:

Cal	Pro	Carb	Fib	Fat	Sat	Chol	Sod
204	27g	4g	<1g	3g	<1g	72mg	543mg

CHICKEN WITH PEPPER AND ONION

TOP OF STOVE

2 chicken breast halves, skinned and boned
1 large onion, thickly sliced and separated into rings
1/2 small green pepper, cut into narrow strips
1/2 small red pepper, cut into narrow strips
1/2 cup sliced fresh mushrooms
Salt and pepper to taste

Place chicken between wax paper and lightly pound to 1/4-inch thickness. Spray a 10-inch non-stick pan with vegetable cooking spray. Heat pan; add chicken and lightly brown, cooking each side about 2 to 3 minutes or until tender and cooked through. Remove from pan and keep warm. Wipe pan with paper towel; spray lightly with vegetable cooking spray. Add onion and cook until slightly softened, stirring frequently. Add peppers and mushrooms. Salt and pepper to taste. Continue cooking until vegetables are cooked, but still slightly crisp. Serve over chicken. Makes 2 servings.

TIP: For 4 servings, cut the same amount of chicken into bite-size chunks or strips. Sauté, stirring frequently, until done. Double the onion, green pepper and mushrooms, add chicken just before serving. This will reduce the fat grams to 2 grams per serving.

Per serving (based on 2 servings):

CAL	PRO	CARB	FIB	FAT	SAT	CHOL	SOD
211	29g	16g	4g	4g	<1g	72mg	68mg

CHICKEN PICANTÉ

TOP OF STOVE

4 chicken breast halves, boned and skinned
1 cup Picanté sauce (mild or medium hot)
1/4 cup water
2 teaspoons freshly grated Parmesan cheese

Place each chicken breast halve between wax paper; pound lightly to an even thickness, about 1/4-inch. Spray medium size non-stick skillet with vegetable cooking spray. Heat until hot. Add chicken and lightly brown both sides. This shouldn't take more than 3 to 4 minutes. Stir in Picanté sauce and water. Bring to a boil, reduce heat, cover and simmer 15 to 20 minutes or until tender, basting occasionally with the sauce. Place chicken on serving plate, top with the sauce. Sprinkle with Parmesan. Makes 4 servings.

Per serving:

CAL	PRO	CARB	FIB	FAT	SAT	CHOL	SOD
170	27g	5g	1g	4g	1g	74mg	398mg

TARRAGON BAKED CHICKEN

OVEN 350°
TOP OF STOVE

1 chicken, cut up, skin removed
1/2 cup flour
1/2 teaspoon dried tarragon (or mixed herbs)
6 tablespoons fresh lemon juice, divided
1/4 cup soft tub margarine
1/4 cup sherry

Combine flour and tarragon. Add chicken pieces to coat. Place, skin-side up, on baking sheet sprayed with vegetable cooking spray. Spoon 4 tablespoons lemon juice over chicken. Bake at 350° for 45 minutes. Meanwhile, in small saucepan, heat the margarine, sherry and remaining 2 tablespoons lemon juice. Heat just until margarine melts; stir to blend. Pour over chicken and continue to cook, basting frequently, 15 minutes or until chicken is tender. Makes 4 servings.

Per serving:

CAL	PRO	CARB	FIB	FAT	SAT	CHOL	SOD
505	51g	14g	<1g	24g	6g	151mg	243mg

CHICKEN ITALIAN

TOP OF STOVE

Dinner in about 30 minutes.

4 chicken breast halves, skinned and boned
1 tablespoon olive oil
1 garlic clove, minced
1 large onion, sliced and separated into rings
1 (14.5-ounce) can Italian stewed tomatoes, with juice
1/4 teaspoon salt (optional)

Lightly brown chicken in non-stick skillet sprayed with vegetable cooking spray. Remove and set aside. Add oil to pan along with the garlic and onion slices. Toss to coat. Cook over medium heat until onion is crisp tender. Stir in tomatoes with juice (cut tomatoes into smaller pieces, if desired) and chicken. Add salt, if desired. Bring to a simmer. Cover and continue to simmer 15 to 20 minutes or until chicken is cooked through and tender. Do not overcook or chicken will be dry. Makes 4 servings.

Per serving:

CAL	PRO	CARB	FIB	FAT	SAT	CHOL	SOD
208	26g	12g	3g	6g	1g	66mg	316mg

EASY BAKED CHICKEN

OVEN 425°

This is so easy it will become a family favorite.

4 chicken breast halves, skinned and boned
1 cup fine fresh bread crumbs
1/2 teaspoon garlic salt
1 teaspoon dried basil, crushed
3/4 teaspoon paprika
1/4 cup egg substitute

Combine bread crumbs, garlic salt, basil and paprika. Dip each chicken breast into egg substitute and then into bread crumb mixture to coat. Place on baking sheet sprayed with vegetable cooking spray. Bake at 425° for 15 minutes. Turn and bake 15 minutes more or until tender. Makes 4 servings.

TIP: For bread crumbs use French bread, sourdough or any other low or no fat bread. Takes about 1 1/2 slices depending on the size of the bread.

Per serving:

CAL	PRO	CARB	FIB	FAT	SAT	CHOL	SOD
178	29g	6g	<1g	4g	1g	72mg	318mg

OVEN SMOTHERED CHICKEN

TOP OF STOVE
OVEN 350°

An easy chicken recipe with a sauce that is very good over rice or mashed potatoes.

4 chicken breast halves, skinned
Salt and pepper
1 1/2 cups chopped onion
1/4 cup flour
2 cups chicken broth

Spray a 10-inch non-stick skillet with vegetable cooking spray. Sprinkle chicken with salt and pepper. Quickly brown chicken on both sides. Remove from skillet. Spray skillet lightly with vegetable cooking spray. Add onions and cook until soft, adding a little water, if necessary to prevent sticking. Stir in flour to blend and coat the onion. Add chicken broth; stir to blend. Cook, over medium heat, until thickened. Taste for seasoning, adding more salt and pepper, if necessary. Place chicken in 2-quart casserole; pour sauce over top. Cover and bake at 350° 40 to 45 minutes or until chicken is cooked through. Makes 4 servings.

Per serving:

CAL	PRO	CARB	FIB	FAT	SAT	CHOL	SOD
196	27g	12g	1g	4g	<1g	66mg	553mg

CHICKEN PINEAPPLE SUPREME

TOP OF STOVE

A beautiful dish for company. They will never know it is a low-fat recipe.

Per Serving:

1 chicken breast half, skinned and boned
Salt and pepper
1 pineapple ring
1 broccoli spear, cooked crisp tender
1/2 slice reduced fat Swiss cheese
Paprika

Place chicken between two pieces of plastic wrap. Gently pound to about 1/4-inch thickness. Place, rounded side down, in a heated non-stick skillet sprayed with vegetable cooking spray. Cook over medium heat, until browned and cooked through, turning once. Total cooking time shouldn't take more than 8 to 10 minutes. Do not overcook. Sprinkle lightly with salt and pepper.

Place a pineapple ring on each chicken breast. Top with broccoli spear. Place a cheese slice diagonally over the broccoli. Sprinkle cheese lightly with paprika. Cover skillet and heat just long enough to melt the cheese. Makes one serving.

TIP: Broccoli spears can be cooked quickly by steaming or cooked in your microwave oven.

Per serving:

CAL	PRO	CARB	FIB	FAT	SAT	CHOL	SOD
270	37g	19g	5g	6g	2g	82mg	138mg

OVEN BAKED CHICKEN WITH YOGURT

OVEN 350°

4 chicken breast halves, skinned
1/2 cup lowfat plain yogurt
1 cup crushed crispy rice cereal
Paprika (optional)

Pat chicken dry with paper towel. Brush generously with yogurt. Dip in crushed cereal to coat. Place, rounded side up, on baking sheet sprayed lightly with vegetable cooking spray. Sprinkle lightly with paprika. Bake at 350° for 50 to 60 minutes or until chicken is tender. Do not overcook or chicken will be dry. Makes 4 servings.

Per serving:

CAL	PRO	CARB	FIB	FAT	SAT	CHOL	SOD
193	29g	10g	0g	4g	1g	74mg	192mg

CHICKEN AND GRAVY

TOP OF STOVE

A nice low fat recipe with gravy.

4 chicken breast halves, skinned
1 cup water, divided
2 tablespoons flour
1/3 cup Lite sour cream
Salt and pepper to taste

Spray a 9 or 10-inch non-stick skillet with vegetable cooking spray. Heat skillet over medium heat; add chicken and quickly brown on both sides. Add 1/2 cup of the water; bring to a boil. Reduce heat; cover and simmer 15 to 20 minutes or until chicken is cooked through. Remove chicken from skillet and keep warm. Place remaining 1/2 cup water in a small jar; add flour and cover. Shake well. Bring water in skillet to a boil; add flour mixture. Cook, stirring constantly until thickened. Remove from heat; stir in sour cream. Season to taste with salt and pepper. Return to heat for a minute, but do not boil. Pour gravy over chicken to serve. Makes 4 servings.

Per serving:

CAL	PRO	CARB	FIB	FAT	SAT	CHOL	SOD
184	29g	4g	0g	6g	3g	82mg	79mg

CHICKEN MEAT LOAF

OVEN 375°

Cold meat loaf, sliced thin, makes great sandwiches.

1 pound boneless chicken breasts
1/2 cup quick-cooking oats
1/2 cup finely chopped onion
1/4 cup finely chopped green pepper
2 egg whites
2/3 cup barbecue sauce, divided

Cut chicken into smaller pieces and place in food processor. With on/off motion, process until chicken is finely ground, but not a mush. Combine with oats, onion, green pepper and 1/3 cup of the barbecue sauce (this may be easier to mix with your hands). Place in 7 x 5-inch loaf pan sprayed with vegetable cooking spray. Bake at 375° (350° if using glass) 40 to 45 minutes or until cooked through. The last 5 minutes of cooking time, spread remaining barbecue sauce over top. Makes 4 servings.

TIP: Use your favorite brand of barbecue sauce or make your own.

Per serving:

CAL	PRO	CARB	FIB	FAT	SAT	CHOL	SOD
227	31g	15g	2g	4g	1g	72mg	431mg

Sweet and Sour Chicken

Top of Stove

One of my favorite ways to serve this is in a hollowed out half pineapple shell with leaves attached. Add small fresh flowers among the leaves. Fill shell with hot cooked rice and top with Sweet and Sour Chicken.

4 chicken breast halves, skinned and boned
1/4 cup white vinegar
1/2 cup firmly packed light brown sugar
1 (20-ounce) can pineapple chunks, save juice
2 tablespoons cornstarch
1/2 red pepper and 1/2 green pepper, cut into narrow strips

Cut chicken into bite-size pieces. Cook over medium-high heat in non-stick skillet sprayed with vegetable cooking spray, until cooked through, stirring frequently. Set aside. In medium saucepan, combine vinegar and brown sugar with 1/2 cup water. Bring to a boil; reduce heat. Drain pineapple. Combine cornstarch with pineapple juice; mix until blended. Stir into saucepan. Add pineapple and peppers. Cook, over low heat, until sauce has thickened and peppers are crisp tender. Makes 6 servings.

Per serving:

Cal	Pro	Carb	Fib	Fat	Sat	Chol	Sod
236	18g	37g	1g	2g	<1g	48mg	50mg

Italian Style Chicken

Top of Stove

Have you ever tried to skin chicken wings? Omit the wings in this recipe and save for homemade chicken broth.

1 chicken cut-up, skin removed
1 (8-ounce) can tomato sauce
1 (14.5 ounce) Italian Style Stewed tomatoes, with juice
1 (4-ounce) can diced green chiles

In large heavy non-stick skillet sprayed with vegetable cooking spray, brown chicken over medium heat, about 15 to 20 minutes. Combine remaining ingredients and pour over chicken. Cover and simmer 15 minutes. Uncover and cook on medium-high, basting chicken frequently, until sauce has thickened and chicken is done. You may need to remove the chicken breasts before the dark meat is cooked through. Makes 6 one piece servings.

Per serving:

Cal	Pro	Carb	Fib	Fat	Sat	Chol	Sod
253	34g	9g	2g	9g	2g	101mg	501mg

BAKED WHOLE CHICKEN

OVEN 325°

An easy way to bake a whole chicken. Serve with stuffing, if desired.

1 (2 - 2½ pound) chicken
Salt and pepper
2 cups water

Place chicken on a rack in large Dutch Oven or high dome roasting pan. Sprinkle lightly with salt and pepper. Add water. Cover and bake at 325° for 2 to 2¼ hours or until almost tender. Uncover. Raise temperature to 400°. Bake 15 minutes or until tender. Remove skin. Makes 6 servings.

Per 4 ounce serving:

CAL	PRO	CARB	FIB	FAT	SAT	CHOL	SOD
324	50g	0g	0g	6g	3g	151mg	146mg

PECAN HERB STUFFING

TOP OF STOVE
OVEN 350°

For best flavor use your favorite brand of seasoned stuffing mix.

1 (7½-ounce) seasoned herb stuffing mix
⅓ cup coarsely chopped pecans
2 tablespoons soft tub margarine
½ cup chopped onion
½ cup chopped celery
1½ cups hot water

In large mixing bowl, combine stuffing mix and pecans. Heat margarine; sauté onion and celery until soft. Add vegetables (along with the margarine) to stuffing mix. Stir in water until well mixed. Pour into 1½ or 2-quart casserole sprayed lightly with vegetable cooking spray. Bake at 350° about 30 minutes or until heated through. Cover for a more moist dressing. Uncover last 10 minutes for a drier dressing. Makes 6 servings.

Per serving:

CAL	PRO	CARB	FIB	FAT	SAT	CHOL	SOD
177	3g	16g	2g	12g	2g	0mg	330mg

Cook's Tip

Watch carefully when sautéing chicken, overcooking will cause the chicken to become dry and tough.

CHICKEN WITH PINEAPPLE

OVEN 350°

1 chicken, cut-up, skin removed
1/2 cup coarsely chopped onion
1 cup pineapple tidbits
1/2 cup pineapple juice
1/2 cup reduced sodium soy sauce
1/2 teaspoon ground ginger

Place chicken pieces in 9x13-inch baking dish sprayed with vegetable cooking spray. Combine remaining ingredients; pour over chicken. Bake at 350° for 60 minutes or until chicken is cooked through, basting frequently with the sauce. Place chicken on serving plate; pour some of the sauce over top. (I remove the pineapple and onion in the sauce.) Makes 4 servings.

Per serving:

CAL	PRO	CARB	FIB	FAT	SAT	CHOL	SOD
487	50g	4g	<1g	13g	3g	151mg	627mg

DIJON CHICKEN KABOBS

BROIL OR GRILL

4 chicken breast halves, skinned and boned
1/3 cup honey
2 tablespoons lemon juice
2 tablespoons Dijon mustard
1/2 teaspoon ground ginger
1 (8 1/4-ounce) can pineapple chunks, drained

Cut chicken into little larger than bite-size chunks (they will shrink). Combine honey, juice, mustard and ginger, mixing to blend. Thread chicken and pineapple on skewers. Brush with Dijon mixture. Broil or grill, about 10 to 12 minutes or until done, turning and brushing frequently with the sauce. Makes 4 servings.

TIP: If using bamboo skewers, you must soak them about 20 minutes in water to prevent burning.

Per serving:

CAL	PRO	CARB	FIB	FAT	SAT	CHOL	SOD
270	27g	34g	<1g	3g	<1g	72mg	163mg

CROCK POT CHICKEN

CROCK POT

1 whole chicken ($2^1/_2$ to 3 pounds)
$^2/_3$ cup coarsely chopped onion
$^1/_2$ cup coarsely chopped celery
$^1/_2$ cup sliced carrots
Salt and pepper

Place chicken in crock pot. Add 2 to 3 cups water along with onion, celery and carrots. Sprinkle with salt and pepper. Cover and cook according to directions for your crock pot. This may take anywhere from 4 to 6 hours. When tender and ready to serve, remove the skin. Makes 4 servings.

Per serving:

CAL	PRO	CARB	FIB	FAT	SAT	CHOL	SOD
345	50g	5g	1g	13g	4g	151mg	173mg

QUICK LEMON PEPPER CHICKEN

OVEN 375°

A very quick way to prepare chicken on those days you don't have time to cook.

4 chicken breast halves, skinned
2 teaspoons olive oil
Lemon pepper

Place chicken on baking pan. Brush with oil. Sprinkle lightly with lemon pepper. Bake at 375° for 40 to 50 minutes or until cooked through. Makes 4 servings.

Per serving:

CAL	PRO	CARB	FIB	FAT	SAT	CHOL	SOD
159	26g	0g	0g	5g	1g	72mg	63mg

GINGER CHICKEN

TOP OF STOVE

A fast and easy way to cook chicken.

4 chicken breast halves, skin removed
1/3 cup reduced sodium soy sauce
2 tablespoons dry sherry
2 tablespoons firmly packed light brown sugar
4 or 5 thin slices fresh ginger (or use 1/2 teaspoon ground ginger)

Add chicken, rounded side down, to 10-inch skillet. Combine remaining ingredients with 1/3 cup water; pour over chicken. Bring sauce to a boil; reduce heat, cover and simmer 10 minutes. Turn chicken, cover and continue to cook 10 minutes. Remove cover; raise heat to medium and cook 5 to 10 minutes, basting frequently until chicken is cooked through and tender. Serve chicken with sauce. Makes 4 servings.

Per serving:

CAL	PRO	CARB	FIB	FAT	SAT	CHOL	SOD
238	26g	7g	0g	3g	<1g	72g	705mg

MAPLE BAKED CHICKEN

TOP OF STOVE
CHILL
OVEN 350°

3/4 cup sugar
1/4 cup firmly packed light brown sugar
1/4 teaspoon Mapeline (a flavoring)
4 chicken breast halves, skin removed
1/2 cup catsup
1/2 cup white wine vinegar

In small saucepan, combine both sugars, Mapeline and 1/2 cup water. Bring to a boil; reduce heat and cook until sugar is dissolved. Chill to thicken sauce. When ready to bake; place the chicken, rounded side down in 9x13-inch baking dish sprayed with vegetable cooking spray. Mix maple sauce with the catsup and vinegar until blended. Pour over chicken. Cover tightly with foil. Bake at 350° for 45 minutes or until tender. Makes 4 servings.

Per serving:

CAL	PRO	CARB	FIB	FAT	SAT	CHOL	SOD
371	27g	61g	<1g	3g	<1g	72mg	431mg

ASHLEY'S CHICKEN

OVEN 350°

Very little sauce clings to the chicken so calorie content is low. The flavor is mild and the chicken is very tender.

4 chicken breast halves, skin removed
1/2 cup orange marmalade
1/2 cup light corn syrup
1 teaspoon freshly grated orange peel

Place chicken, rounded-side down, in shallow baking pan sprayed with vegetable cooking spray. Bake at 350° for 30 minutes. Combine marmalade, corn syrup and orange peel. Turn chicken; brush with some of the sauce. Cook 30 minutes, or until chicken is tender, basting every 10 minutes with sauce. Makes 4 servings.

TIP: If you prefer the chicken a little darker in color, baste last 10 minutes with sauce from the pan.

Per serving:

CAL	PRO	CARB	FIB	FAT	SAT	CHOL	SOD
251	27g	29g	<1g	3g	<1g	72mg	81mg

LEMON CHICKEN

MARINATE
OVEN 350°

4 chicken breast halves, skin removed
2 large lemons (you will need 1/2 cup juice)
1/2 cup flour
3/4 teaspoon salt
1/4 teaspoon freshly ground black pepper
4 1/2 teaspoons soft tub margarine, melted

Place chicken, breast side down, in 8 x 8-inch dish. Squeeze juice from lemons; pour over top. Place in refrigerator and marinate 1 hour or longer, if desired, basting occasionally with the juice. Combine flour, salt and pepper. Coat chicken with flour mixture. Place on baking sheet sprayed with vegetable cooking spray. Drizzle margarine over top. Bake at 350° for 50 to 60 minutes or until cooked through and chicken starts to brown. If chicken isn't browning, baste with some of the drippings in pan. Makes 4 servings.

Per serving:

CAL	PRO	CARB	FIB	FAT	SAT	CHOL	SOD
235	28g	12g	<1g	7g	2g	72mg	499mg

LEMON PEPPER CHICKEN

OVEN 350°

A simple but tasty dish

4 chicken breast halves, skin removed
Lemon pepper
1 lemon
Parsley

Place chicken in 8 x 8-inch baking dish sprayed with vegetable cooking spray. Sprinkle lightly with lemon pepper. Cut lemon into 8 slices. Place two slices on each chicken breast. Sprinkle with parsley. Bake at 350° (325° if using glass dish) for 45 to 60 minutes or until chicken is cooked through and tender. Makes 4 servings.

Per serving:

CAL	PRO	CARB	FIB	FAT	SAT	CHOL	SOD
140	26g	<1g	<1g	3g	<1g	72mg	63mg

LAURA'S FAVORITE CHICKEN LEGS

MARINATE
OVEN 350°

When my granddaughter, Laura, asked for seconds, I knew I had a winner.

8 chicken legs
1/2 cup catsup
1/4 cup sugar
3 tablespoons white vinegar
2 tablespoons pineapple juice
2 tablespoons reduced sodium soy sauce

Place chicken in 8 x 8-inch dish. Combine remaining ingredients and pour over chicken. Cover; place in refrigerator and marinate several hours or overnight, turning chicken several times. Remove chicken from marinade; place on baking pan sprayed with vegetable cooking spray. Brush with sauce. Bake at 350° for 50 to 60 minutes or until cooked through, brushing several times with the remaining sauce. Makes 8 servings.

TIP: Remove skin before eating (flavor will still remain).

Per leg:

CAL	PRO	CARB	FIB	FAT	SAT	CHOL	SOD
130	13g	11g	<1g	3g	<1g	41mg	344mg

CHICKEN IN A BAG

OVEN 375°

So easy! Put the ingredients in the bag, place in oven and forget about it until chicken is done and vegetables are tender.

1 large plastic oven cooking bag (14 x 20-inch)
2 tablespoons flour
1 teaspoon seasoning salt, divided
4 medium potatoes, peeled
8 medium carrots, cut in half crosswise
1 chicken, cut up (about 2 1/2 pounds)

Place bag in 9 x 13-inch baking dish. Add flour, 1 teaspoon of the seasoning salt and 1/3 cup water to bag. Squeeze or shake to mix thoroughly. Add vegetables, turning to coat. Arrange vegetables in one layer. Sprinkle chicken with remaining seasoning salt. Place on top of vegetables in one layer, skin side up. Close opening of bag tightly with twist. Cut 6 or 7 small slits in top of bag. Bake at 375° for 55 to 60 minutes or until cooked through. Carefully remove skin before eating. Makes 4 servings.

TIP: Oven bag cooking is easy and the food is so moist and tender, I'm surprised we don't use this method of cooking more often.

Per serving:

CAL	PRO	CARB	FIB	FAT	SAT	CHOL	SOD
507	53g	42g	6g	13g	4g	151mg	497mg

CHICKEN N' PEACHES

OVEN 350°

You can have this in the oven in less than 10 minutes.

4 chicken breast halves, skinned
1/4 cup reduced sodium soy sauce
1/4 cup honey
2 tablespoons chili sauce
3/4 teaspoon ground ginger
1 (16-ounce) can peach halves, drained

Combine soy sauce, honey, chili sauce and ginger; mix thoroughly. Place chicken, rounded side down, on shallow baking pan sprayedwith cooking spray. Lightly brush both sides of chicken with sauce. Bake at 350° for 30 minutes. Turn chicken, brush with sauce, and bake 20 to 25 minutes or until chicken is tender, basting about every 5 minutes with sauce. Add peach halves the last 10 minutes of baking time. Makes 4 servings.

Per serving:

CAL	PRO	CARB	FIB	FAT	SAT	CHOL	SOD
314	27g	40g	2g	3g	<1g	72mg	663mg

CHICKEN TORTILLA TURNOVERS

OVEN 450°

For each turnover you will need:

1 (8-inch) flour tortilla
2 ounces cooked cubed chicken
3 tablespoons salsa (well drained)
1/4 cup (1 ounce) reduced fat Cheddar cheese, shredded

Place tortilla on baking sheet. Arrange chicken evenly over half of the tortilla. Top with salsa. Sprinkle evenly with cheese. Place in 450° oven and bake about a minute or until cheese is melted. Watch carefully, you don't want the tortilla to crisp. Remove from oven. Fold tortilla in half like a turnover, pressing edges to seal.

VARIATION: Fill tortilla with chicken, 2 tablespoons chopped plum tomatoes, 1 tablespoon chopped onion, sprinkle with cheese. Bake as above; fold and serve topped with salsa. Can also use leftover Chicken Fajitas with Onion & Peppers (page 123) as a filling.

Per turnover:

CAL	PRO	CARB	FIB	FAT	SAT	CHOL	SOD
295	29g	22g	2g	11g	4g	68mg	428mg

ONE DISH CHICKEN DINNER

OVEN 350°

Easy, healthy, colorful and good. A quick busy day meal.

4 chicken breast halves, skin removed
8 small new potatoes (about 1 pound)
4 medium carrots
2 cups chicken broth
Salt and pepper
1/2 pound fresh green beans, cooked

Wash potatoes, but do not peel; cut in half and place, cut side up, in 9 x 13-inch pan sprayed with vegetable cooking spray. Cut carrots in half crosswise, then lengthwise. Scatter among potatoes. Pour broth over vegetables. Place chicken on top. Sprinkle with salt and coarsely ground black pepper. Cover with foil. Bake at 350° (325° if using glass) for 60 minutes. Remove foil; baste chicken with broth. Add green beans to dish. Bake 15 minutes or until beans are heated through. Makes 4 servings.

TIP: The chicken doesn't brown in this recipe so if this bothers you, sprinkle chicken with a little paprika before baking. If you can't find good fresh green beans in the market, use one 16-ounce can green beans, drained.

CAL	PRO	CARB	FIB	FAT	SAT	CHOL	SOD
377	32g	55g	4g	4g	<1g	66mg	746mg

SWISS ONION CHICKEN

OVEN 350°

It would be hard to find a chicken recipe easier than this one. Dinner can be ready in less than 45 minutes.

4 chicken breast halves, skinned and boned
Salt (optional)
2 tablespoons Dijon mustard
3 green onions
½ cup (2-ounces) reduced fat Swiss cheese, shredded
Paprika

Place chicken, rounded side up, in shallow baking pan sprayed with vegetable cooking spray. If desired, sprinkle lightly with salt. Brush mustard over chicken. Slice onions; sprinkle over chicken. Sprinkle evenly with cheese. Sprinkle lightly with paprika. Bake at 350° for 20 to 25 minutes or until chicken is cooked through. Makes 4 servings.

Per serving:

CAL	PRO	CARB	FIB	FAT	SAT	CHOL	SOD
201	31g	2g	<1g	7g	3g	85mg	199mg

EASY MOCK CHICKEN CORDON BLEU

OVEN 350°

Most of us enjoy Cordon Bleu, but lack the time or patience to prepare it as often as we would like. With just ¼ ounce of cheese per serving, you won't be going over your fat allowance.

4 chicken breast halves, skinned and boned
1 cup fresh bread crumbs
1½ teaspoons seasoning salt
4 tablespoons nonfat yogurt
4 thin slices boiled ham
1 thin slice Swiss cheese, about 5x8-inches, cut into 4 rectangles

Wash chicken and pat dry. Combine bread crumbs and seasoning salt. Brush each chicken breast with 1 tablespoon yogurt. Roll in crumbs to coat. Place on baking sheet sprayed with vegetable cooking spray. Bake at 350° for 30 to 40 minutes or until cooked through. Remove from oven; top each chicken breast with a ham slice folded to form a rectangle. Top with a slice of cheese. Return to oven and bake until cheese is melted. Makes 4 servings.

TIP: If desired, sprinkle with a little chopped parsley for added color, or garnish each serving with a sprig of parsley.

Per serving:

CAL	PRO	CARB	FIB	FAT	SAT	CHOL	SOD
207	33g	6g	<1g	5g	1g	86g	1059g

CHICKEN FINGERS

TOP OF STOVE

A light luncheon dish. For dinner servings add 4 more chicken tenderloins or 1/2 chicken breast.

8 chicken tenderloins (or 3 chicken breast halves, boned skinned and cut into 8 pieces)
1 teaspoon olive oil
1 1/2 cups chunky garden style spaghetti sauce
8 ounces spaghetti, cooked
1 tablespoon grated Parmesan cheese

Quickly brown chicken in hot oil in non-stick skillet. Add spaghetti sauce. Lower heat and simmer 3 to 5 minutes or until chicken is tender. Serve over spaghetti. Sprinkle each serving with 3/4 teaspoon grated Parmesan. Makes 4 servings.

TIP: Chicken tenderloins can often be found frozen in 3 pound size bags.

Per serving:

CAL	PRO	CARB	FIB	FAT	SAT	CHOL	SOD
453	29g	63g	<1g	8g	1g	50mg	456mg

Cook's Tip

Sautéing

To limit fat in cooking, start by sautéing foods in a very small amount of fat. When it looks like you may need more oil, add chicken broth or water instead.

LEMON CHICKEN PACKETS

OVEN 375°

Chicken can be baked in individual packets and served from the containers.

Per person:

1 chicken breast half, skinned
1 tablespoon lemon juice
Dried tarragon or rosemary
Salt and pepper
1 green onion, sliced

Place chicken on a square of foil. Pour lemon juice over top. Sprinkle lightly with tarragon, salt and pepper. Sprinkle with green onion. Cover chicken with foil and seal. Place on shallow baking pan. Bake at 375° for 45 to 60 minutes or until cooked through. Makes 1 serving.

TIP: Smaller chicken breasts will usually cook in 45 minutes and larger ones will take 60 minutes.

Per serving:

CAL	PRO	CARB	FIB	FAT	SAT	CHOL	SOD
147	27g	2g	<1g	3g	<1g	72mg	278mg

ROAST CHICKEN IN FOIL

OVEN 400°

1 whole chicken, about 3 1/2 pounds
1/2 teaspoon salt
1/4 teaspoon pepper
1/4 teaspoon garlic powder
1/4 teaspoon dried rosemary

Place chicken on a large piece of foil. Combine remaining ingredients. Sprinkle mixture evenly on inside and over outside of chicken. Wrap foil around chicken to seal. Place in a shallow baking pan. Bake at 400° for 1 hour. Reduce heat to 350° and continue to cook 30 minutes or until chicken is cooked through. Chicken should be tender and moist. Open foil; carefully remove the chicken skin. Makes 4 to 6 servings.

Per 3 ounce serving:

CAL	PRO	CARB	FIB	FAT	SAT	CHOL	SOD
164	25g	<1g	<1g	6g	2g	76mg	340mg

SKINNY CHICKEN WITH FRUIT

TOP OF STOVE

A quick and easy recipe to make on those days when you want to greatly reduce the fat content of your meal. Served with a sourdough roll or toasted bagel half, this makes a very satisfying and filling lunch or dinner.

Per serving:

1 chicken breast half, skinned and boned
2 wedges watermelon
3 thin slices cantaloupe
4 large strawberries
Lettuce leaf

Pat chicken dry; trim off any fat. Place between waxed paper. Pound lightly until even and about 1/4-inch thick. Place in heated non-stick skillet sprayed with vegetable cooking spray. Cook about 2 to 3 minutes per side or until cooked through, this won't take long. (See tip below.) Place chicken on dinner plate. Arrange fruit on lettuce leaf. Makes 1 serving.

TIP: To keep the chicken from drying out and for added flavor, it can be brushed or basted with one of the following:

1 teaspoon reduced calorie Italian dressing
Chicken broth
Teriyaki sauce
Sprinkle of lemon pepper.

Per serving:

CAL	PRO	CARB	FIB	FAT	SAT	CHOL	SOD
291	30g	35g	6g	5g	1g	72mg	82mg

CHICKEN FRIED RICE

TOP OF STOVE

You must use cold rice in this recipe.

3 chicken breast halves, skinned and boned
2 teaspoons Canola oil
1/2 cup egg substitute
4 cups cooked rice, chilled
3 green onions, sliced
2 tablespoons reduced sodium soy sauce

Cut chicken into bite-size pieces. Heat oil in large non-stick skillet or wok. Add chicken; cook quickly over high heat until tender, stirring frequently. Remove chicken. Add egg substitute; cook until scrambled. Return chicken to skillet along with the rice and onion. Cook, over medium heat, stirring frequently until rice is heated through. Stir in soy sauce. Makes 4 main dish servings.

Per serving:

CAL	PRO	CARB	FIB	FAT	SAT	CHOL	SOD
404	28g	58g	<1g	5g	<1g	54mg	93mg

PEPPER'S CHICKEN WITH FRUIT

OVEN 350°

4 chicken breast halves, skin removed
Garlic salt
Fresh ground black pepper
4 onion slices
4 green pepper slices
1 (16-ounce) can Lite chunky mixed fruits, with juice

Place chicken breasts, rounded side up, in 9 x 13-inch baking dish sprayed with vegetable cooking spray. Sprinkle lightly with garlic salt and ground pepper. Top each with an onion slice and a green pepper slice. Pour fruit and juice on and around the chicken. Cover with foil; bake at 350° (325° if using glass baking dish) for 60 minutes. Remove foil; increase heat to 375°. Bake 15 to 20 minutes, basting frequently, until chicken is tender. Makes 4 servings.

Per serving:

CAL	PRO	CARB	FIB	FAT	SAT	CHOL	SOD
201	27g	16g	2g	3g	<1g	72mg	202mg

HONEY BAKED CHICKEN

OVEN 350°

An odd combination of flavors I think you will enjoy.

4 chicken breast halves, skinned and boned
1/4 cup honey
1 tablespoon reduced sodium soy sauce
2 tablespoons chicken broth
1/2 teaspoon chili powder

Place chicken breasts in 8 x 8-inch baking dish sprayed with vegetable cooking spray. Combine remaining ingredients until well mixed. Pour over chicken. Bake at 350° (325° if using glass dish) for 45 minutes, basting occasionally, until chicken is tender. Makes 4 servings.

Per serving:

CAL	PRO	CARB	FIB	FAT	SAT	CHOL	SOD
218	27g	18g	<1g	3g	<1g	72mg	218mg

CHICKEN WRAP-UPS

OVEN 350°

A nice little bundle that will delight your guests.

For each serving:

1 chicken breast half, skinned and boned
1 thin slice deli boiled ham
1 strip thin sliced Swiss cheese, about 1 1/2 x 2 1/2-inches
1 1/2 teaspoon Light cream cheese product
1 strip of bacon

Place chicken breast between waxed pepper. Pound lightly until even and about 1/4-inch thick. Roll up ham slice and place in center of chicken, but closer to one end. Top with Swiss cheese. Spread cream cheese over top. Roll up chicken to completely enclose filling. Use wooden toothpicks to close if necessary. Wrap bacon around chicken. Place on baking pan. Bake at 350° for 40 to 45 minutes or until chicken is cooked through. Makes 1 serving.

TIP: Make sure ends of roll are sealed to prevent melted cheese from spilling out. If desired, remove bacon before eating.

Per serving:

CAL	PRO	CARB	FIB	FAT	SAT	CHOL	SOD
281	39g	1g	0g	13g	6g	106mg	646mg

HAWAIIAN SKILLET CHICKEN

TOP OF STOVE

A colorful chicken recipe served over cooked rice.

1 chicken, cut up
Seasoning salt
1 1/2 green peppers (could use half red and half green) cut into strips
1 (20-ounce) can pineapple chunks, drain and save 1/4 cup juice
4 ounces fresh mushrooms, sliced

Sprinkle chicken pieces lightly with seasoning salt. Brown in large deep non-stick skillet, sprayed with vegetable cooking spray. Pour off any fat that may accumulate. Add remaining ingredients including the 1/4 cup juice. Cover; reduce heat and simmer 60 minutes or until chicken is cooked through. Remove skin before serving. Makes 4 to 6 servings.

Per 3 ounce serving:

CAL	PRO	CARB	FIB	FAT	SAT	CHOL	SOD
295	34g	20g	2g	9g	2g	101mg	189mg

CHICKEN WITH ORANGE SAUCE

TOP OF STOVE

A quick recipe you can do in less than 30 minutes.

4 chicken breast halves, skinned and boned
1 teaspoon olive oil
4 oranges
2 tablespoons firmly packed light brown sugar
1/8 teaspoon salt
2 1/2 teaspoons cornstarch

Heat oil in medium non-stick skillet. Quickly brown chicken in hot oil. Reduce heat. Add about 1/4 cup water; cover and cook 6 to 7 minutes or until chicken is cooked through. Don't overcook or chicken will be tough and dry. Remove chicken and keep warm. Pour off any remaining liquid in skillet and wipe skillet clean with a paper towel.

Squeeze 3/4 cup juice from the oranges. Combine brown sugar, salt and cornstarch; stir to blend. Combine orange juice and sugar mixture. Pour into skillet; cook over medium heat until mixture boils and thickens, stirring frequently. Pour sauce over chicken. Makes 4 servings.

TIP: If desired, add 1/2 teaspoon grated orange peel to the sauce.

Per serving:

CAL	PRO	CARB	FIB	FAT	SAT	CHOL	SOD
206	27	14	<1g	4g	1g	72mg	146mg

Marinated Chicken Strips

MARINATE
TOP OF STOVE

This quick and easy marinade gives the chicken a wonderful mild ginger flavor. No additional oil is necessary for stir-frying.

1 pound boneless chicken breast
2 teaspoons Canola oil
1/4 teaspoon salt
4 to 5 thin slices fresh ginger

Cut chicken into small cubes or strips. In small bowl combine chicken with remaining ingredients. Cover and chill at least 1 hour or more. To stir-fry, remove ginger slices. Place in large non-stick skillet over medium-high heat. Cook quickly, stirring often, until lightly browned and cooked through. Do not overcook or chicken will be tough. Makes 4 servings.

TIP: Chicken can be used in salads, stir-fry, pizza, etc.

Per serving:

CAL	PRO	CARB	FIB	FAT	SAT	CHOL	SOD
160	26g	0g	0g	5g	1g	72mg	196mg

Cook's Tip

We used to think fat and carbohydrate calories were equal, but that isn't true.

One gram of fat = 9 calories
One gram of carb. = 4 calories

STUFFED CHICKEN BREASTS PINEAPPLE

OVEN 350°

Impress your guests with these pineapple stuffed chicken rolls.

4 chicken breast halves, skinned and boned
4 teaspoons Dijon mustard
1/2 cup Angel Flake coconut
4 pineapple spears
3 tablespoons nonfat plain yogurt
3/4 cup fresh bread crumbs

Place each chicken breast half between waxed paper; lightly pound to 1/4-inch thickness. Spread each with 1 teaspoon mustard; sprinkle with 2 tablespoons coconut. Place pineapple spear near one end. Fold end over spear, fold sides in about 1 inch. Roll to enclose pineapple. If chicken won't stay sealed, secure with toothpicks. Brush with yogurt. Roll in crumbs to coat. Place on baking sheet sprayed with vegetable cooking spray. Lightly spray rolls with cooking spray. Bake at 350° for 45 to 50 minutes or until cooked through and golden. Makes 4 servings.

Per serving:

CAL	PRO	CARB	FIB	FAT	SAT	CHOL	SOD
224	29g	12g	2g	7g	4g	73mg	203mg

CHICKEN RICE DISH

OVEN 350°

A nice busy day casserole.

1 chicken, cut up
Seasoning salt
1 cup uncooked long grain rice
4 ounces fresh mushrooms, sliced
1/4 cup finely chopped onion
2 1/4 cups chicken broth

Sprinkle chicken pieces lightly with seasoning salt. Place rice in 11 x 7-inch baking dish sprayed with vegetable cooking spray. Add mushrooms, onion and broth. Stir ingredients to distribute evenly in dish. Arrange chicken, skin-side up, on top. Cover with foil. Bake at 350° for 60 to 75 minutes or until liquid is absorbed. Remove foil last 15 minutes of cooking time. Remove skin before eating. Makes 4 servings.

Per serving:

CAL	PRO	CARB	FIB	FAT	SAT	CHOL	SOD
362	30g	40g	1g	8g	2g	76mg	637mg

NICE 'N TENDER CHICKEN

OVEN 350°

An old family recipe that fits into today's life style.

1 chicken, cut up
Seasoning salt
1 tablespoon flour
2 cups hot chicken broth

Sprinkle chicken lightly with seasoning salt. Sprinkle flour over bottom of 8 x 8-inch baking dish. Place chicken in dish, skin-side down. Pour hot chicken broth carefully into dish. Bake at 350° (325° if using glass dish) for 45 minutes or until chicken is golden brown and tender. Remove skin before eating. Makes 6 servings.

Per serving:

CAL	PRO	CARB	FIB	FAT	SAT	CHOL	SOD
232	34g	2g	<1g	9g	2g	101mg	429mg

BARBECUE CHICKEN

OVEN 350°

For children, substitute chicken legs for the chicken breasts.

4 chicken breast halves, skinned
1/2 cup barbecue sauce
2 tablespoons fresh orange juice
1 teaspoon grated orange peel
2 tablespoons honey

Place chicken, skin-side up, in shallow baking pan sprayed generously with vegetable cooking spray. Combine remaining ingredients. Brush chicken lightly with some of the sauce. Bake at 350° for 50 to 60 minutes, basting every 15 minutes with remaining sauce, until cooked through. Makes 4 servings.

Per serving:

CAL	PRO	CARB	FIB	FAT	SAT	CHOL	SOD
199	27g	14g	<1g	4g	<1g	72mg	32mg

ORANGE GLAZED TURKEY BREAST

OVEN 325°

The marmalade glaze is wonderful and the black pepper makes for an attractive touch to the finished product.

6 pound whole turkey breast
1/2 teaspoon olive oil
1/2 cup orange marmalade
1 tablespoon prepared mustard
2 teaspoons Worcestershire sauce
1/2 teaspoon fresh coarsely ground black pepper or cracked pepper

Clean turkey breast, trimming off all loose pieces of skin, etc. Pat dry. Place, breast-side u,p on rack in roasting pan. Brush with oil. Cover with foil or roasting pan lid. Bake at 350° for 1 1/2 hours. Combine remaining ingredients. Remove cover from turkey; baste with sauce and continue cooking 30 to 45 minutes or until temperature reaches 180°, basting frequently with the sauce. Cover; let stand 15 minutes before slicing. Makes approximately eighteen 3 ounce servings.

TIP: I like to do this recipe in my electric covered roaster - it always seems to come out so moist and evenly browned.

Per 3 ounce serving:

CAL	PRO	CARB	FIB	FAT	SAT	CHOL	SOD
149	28g	6g	<1g	1g	<1g	78mg	62mg

BAKED TURKEY TENDERLOINS

OVEN 350°

If you happen to have bought turkey tenderloins and don't know what to do with them, try this very quick and easy recipe.

2 (8-ounce) turkey tenderloins or breast fillets
2 teaspoons olive oil
Paprika
Salt
Freshly ground pepper

Place tenderloins, rounded-side up, on baking sheet. Brush each with 1 teaspoon oil. Sprinkle lightly with paprika, salt and pepper. Bake at 350° for 30 to 35 minutes or until cooked through. Do not overcook or turkey will be tough and dry. Cut into diagonal slices. Makes 4 servings.

Per serving:

CAL	PRO	CARB	FIB	FAT	SAT	CHOL	SOD
140	26g	.2g	0	3g	.6g	73mg	181mg

TURKEY STOVETOP DINNER

TOP OF STOVE

This is a nice dish for small children who are on solid foods. The turkey is very tender and easy for them to eat.

1 pound raw turkey breast slices
1 cup chopped onion
1 cup salsa (mild to hot depending on taste)
1 (16-ounce) can tomatoes, cut up
1 (12-ounce) can Mexican corn
1½ cups quick-cooking rice

Cut turkey breast into chunks. Put in food processor and process until cut up fine, but not a paste. Spray a deep non-stick 10-inch skillet with vegetable cooking spray. Sauté turkey until cooked through. Add remaining ingredients along with 1 cup water. Bring to a boil and cook about 2 minutes. Turn off heat; cover and let stand 5 minutes. Makes 6 servings.

Per serving:

CAL	PRO	CARB	FIB	FAT	SAT	CHOL	SOD
262	24g	36g	3g	3g	.5g	57mg	353mg

TURKEY-BACON BURGERS

TOP OF STOVE

The bacon keeps the patties moist and adds a lot of flavor.

1 pound lean ground turkey
¾ cup fresh whole wheat bread crumbs
2 egg whites
1 tablespoon Worcestershire sauce
Salt and pepper to taste
6 slices lean bacon

In large mixing bowl, combine the first five ingredients. Gently mix thoroughly. (This is easier to do with your hands.) Form into 6 patties. Carefully wrap a strip of bacon around outside of each patty; fasten with a wooden toothpick. Cook patties in nonstick skillet, under a broiler or on a grill, until cooked through. Do not overcook. Remove bacon and discard. Makes 6 servings.

TIP: I find, in most cases, the bacon is not completely cooked through (crisp) by the time the burger is done. A good reason not to eat all that extra fat, but still enjoy the flavor.

Per burger:

CAL	PRO	CARB	FIB	FAT	SAT	CHOL	SOD
122	15g	<1g	0g	5g	na	na	na

TACO TURKEY BURGER PATTIES

TOP OF STOVE

I cooked the turkey burgers in a non-stick skillet with raised edges like a grill. Not one drop of fat or water remained in the skillet even though the turkey was listed as 93% fat free (41% fat). Also, there wasn't any shrinkage.

1 1/2 pounds lean ground turkey
1 (1 1/4-ounce) package taco seasoning mix
1/3 cup fine fresh bread crumbs
2 egg whites

Combine ingredients in medium mixing bowl. Mix lightly to blend. This may be easier to do with your hands. Divide and shape into 8 patties a little thicker than 1/4-inch and about the size of hamburger buns. The shaping is easier to do if you wet your hands with a little water. Place in non-stick skillet, on grill, or under broiler. Cook until lightly browned and cooked through. This may take 3 to 4 minutes on each side. Makes 8 patties.

Per pattie:

CAL	PRO	CARB	FIB	FAT	SAT	CHOL	SOD
129	18g	2g	0g	6g	na	na	na

TERIYAKI TURKEY BURGERS

GRILL

Delicious served on a hamburger bun with a pineapple slice and lettuce.

1 pound lean ground turkey
3 tablespoons reduced sodium soy sauce
2 teaspoons pineapple juice
1/4 cup fine fresh bread crumbs
1/8 teaspoon ground ginger

Combine all the ingredients, mixing well to blend. (I find this easier to do if I use my hands.) Form into 6 patties. Cook in a non-stick skillet, or broil or grill, until cooked through. Makes 6 servings.

Per serving:

CAL	PRO	CARB	FIB	FAT	SAT	CHOL	SOD
126	14g	2g	0g	5g	na	na	na

THE EASIEST LASAGNA

TOP OF STOVE
CHILL, OVEN 350°

Not necessary to boil the noodles, but has to be assembled the night before.

1 pound lean ground turkey
1 (30-ounce) jar chunky spaghetti sauce with mushrooms and onions
1 (16-ounce) container low fat cottage cheese
1/2 teaspoon oregano
8 ounces uncooked lasagna noodles
16 ounces Lite Mozzarella cheese, shredded

Brown turkey in medium skillet; drain. Add spaghetti sauce and 1 cup water. Bring to a boil, reduce heat and simmer about 5 minutes. Lightly spray 9 x 13-inch pan with vegetable cooking spray. Spread **1 1/2** cups sauce on bottom. Arrange half the uncooked noodles on sauce. Spread with half the cottage cheese. Sprinkle with half the oregano and half the Mozzarella. Repeat layers with remaining ingredients. Cover with foil; refrigerate overnight.

Uncover; bake at 350° for 50 to 60 minutes or until noodles are tender and cheese is lightly golden. Remove from oven; let stand 10 to 15 minutes before serving (to absorb any remaining liquid in the pan). Makes 12 servings.

Per serving:

CAL	PRO	CARB	FIB	FAT	SAT	CHOL	SOD
303	26g	29g	<1g	9g	na	na	>669

PEPPER PASTA WITH TURKEY

TOP OF STOVE

A very tasty and colorful pasta dish.

8 ounces wide Fettuccine noodles
1 tablespoon Canola oil
$1^1/_2$ cups coarsely chopped onion
2 medium peppers, 1 green and 1 red (you will need 2 cups diced)
1 pound lean ground turkey
Salt and pepper to taste

Cook noodles according to package directions; drain. Meanwhile heat oil in large non-stick skillet. Add onion; cook 2 to 3 minutes, stirring frequently. Add diced peppers; cook until vegetables are just crisp tender. Remove from skillet. Add turkey and lightly brown. Pour off any remaining liquid. Return vegetables and quickly heat through. Toss mixture with hot noodles (it may be necessary to put mixture in a large mixing bowl if skillet is too full for tossing.) Season to taste with salt and pepper. Makes 6 servings.

Per serving:

CAL	PRO	CARB	FIB	FAT	SAT	CHOL	SOD
294	20g	40g	<1g	8g	na	na	na

TURKEY BROCCOLI LOAF

TOP OF STOVE
OVEN 350°

An easy way to get the kids to eat their broccoli.

$1^1/_2$ pounds lean ground turkey
$1^1/_4$ cups quick cooking oats
1 cup finely chopped onion
2 egg whites
Salt and pepper, to taste
1 cup broccoli flowerettes, coarsely chopped

Place first 5 ingredients in large mixing bowl. Microwave or steam broccoli. This will take about a minute in the microwave. Don't overcook; broccoli should still be quite firm. Add to turkey along with $^1/_4$ cup water. Mix, with hands, until thoroughly blended. Spoon into 8 x4-inch loaf pan sprayed with vegetable cooking spray. Bake at 350° (325° if using glass) for 60 minutes or until cooked through. The loaf should feel rather firm to the touch. Remove from pan, cover with foil and let stand 10 minutes for easier slicing. Makes 8 servings.

Per serving:

CAL	PRO	CARB	FIB	FAT	SAT	CHOL	SOD
127	15g	7g	1g	5g	na	na	na

PAULINA'S FAVORITE TURKEY MEATBALLS

OVEN 400°

A versatile meatball. Broken into smaller pieces it makes nice finger food for small children. My little granddaughter, Paulina, enjoyed these before (and after) she got her first molars.

1 pound lean ground turkey
1/2 cup fine fresh bread crumbs
2 egg whites
2 tablespoons finely chopped onion
1/2 teaspoon prepared horseradish
1/2 teaspoon salt

In mixing bowl, combine all the ingredients, mixing to blend (this may be easier to do with your hands). Shape into walnut-size meatballs. Place in shallow baking pan sprayed with vegetable cooking spray. Bake at 400° for 18 to 20 minutes or until cooked through. Makes 24 meatballs.

TIP: For convenience, make several recipes at one time and freeze.

Per meatball:

CAL	PRO	CARB	FIB	FAT	SAT	CHOL	SOD
24	3g	<1g	<1g	1g	na	na	na

PIZZA TURKEY LOAF

OVEN 350°

2 pounds lean ground turkey
1 cup fine fresh bread crumbs
1 cup finely chopped onion
2 egg whites
1 (15 1/2-ounce) jar pizza sauce, divided
2 cups (8-ounces) Lite Mozzarella cheese, shredded, divided

Place first 4 ingredients in large mixing bowl. Add all but 1/2 cup pizza sauce and 2/3 cup Mozzarella. Mix, with hands, until blended. Spoon into 9″x5″ loaf pan sprayed with vegetable cooking spray.. Bake at 350° (325° if using glass) for 45 minutes. Spread reserved pizza sauce over top. Bake 15 minutes. Sprinkle cheese over top and bake 15 minutes or until cooked through. With the sauce and cheese, it is a little hard to see if the loaf is done, but it should feel quite firm to the touch. Carefully pour off liquid. Cover with foil; let stand 10 minutes for easier slicing. Makes 10 servings.

Per serving:

CAL	PRO	CARB	FIB	FAT	SAT	CHOL	SOD
214	27g	8g	<1g	9g	na	na	na

TURKEY GOULASH

TOP OF STOVE

1 pound lean ground turkey
1 cup chopped onion
1 cup chopped celery
2 (14.5-ounce) cans tomatoes with juice, cut into smaller pieces
5 ounces noodles, cooked
Salt and pepper to taste

Spray 10-inch skillet with vegetable cooking spray. Cook turkey over medium-high heat, stirring frequently, until almost cooked through. Stir in onion and celery. Cover; cook over low heat until soft, stirring occasionally to prevent sticking. Add tomatoes. Add salt and pepper to taste. Bring to a boil; reduce heat and simmer 15 minutes. Meanwhile, cook noodles according to package directions. Add drained noodles to meat mixture. Cook until heated through. Makes 6 servings.

Per serving:

CAL	PRO	CARB	FIB	FAT	SAT	CHOL	SOD
223	17g	30g	2g	5g	na	na	na

Cook's Tip

Handling Poultry

To prevent unwanted bacteria growth, always rinse poultry and pat dry before starting preparation. Wash hands and any surface coming in contact with raw chicken. Do not allow uncooked chicken to stand at room temperture.

TURKEY SAUSAGE SPAGHETTI SAUCE

TOP OF STOVE

The sugar smooths out the acidity of the tomatoes. I doubt if you can taste it, but it does enhance the flavor of the sauce.

3/4 pound turkey sausage links
1/2 cup chopped onion
1 (28-ounce) can whole tomatoes, with juice
1 (8-ounce) can tomato sauce
1 teaspoon Italian seasoning
1 teaspoon sugar

Cut each sausage link crosswise into 6 pieces. Cook sausage and onion in nonstick skillet until sausage is browned and onion is soft. Pour off any liquid. Cut tomatoes into small pieces; add to skillet along with the juice and remaining ingredients. Bring to a boil; reduce heat and simmer about 60 minutes or until sauce has thickened. Serve over spaghetti. Makes 4 cups.

Per 1/2 cup serving:

CAL	PRO	CARB	FIB	FAT	SAT	CHOL	SOD
113	4g	8g	2g	6g	2g	22mg	347mg

With 2 ounces spaghetti:

CAL	PRO	CARB	FIB	FAT	SAT	CHOL	SOD
371	13g	61g	2g	7g	2g	22mg	347mg

LASAGNA ROLLS

TOP OF STOVE
OVEN 350°

A new twist to a family favorite.

12 lasagna noodles
$1^1/_2$ pounds lean ground chicken
1 (32-ounce) jar chunky spaghetti sauce with mushroom and tomato
2 cups (8-ounces) Lite Mozzarella, shredded

Cook noodles according to package directions. Quickly rinse noodles to prevent them from sticking. Meanwhile, brown chicken in non-stick skillet; pour off liquid. Stir in spaghetti sauce. Bring to a boil; reduce heat and simmer about 5 minutes. Lay a noodle on flat surface, sprinkle with a small amount of cheese (not more than a tablespoon). Cover with about 2 tablespoons sauce. Carefully roll up. Place, spiral side up, in 8x8-inch baking dish sprayed with non-stick cooking spray. Repeat with remaining noodles. Spread remaining sauce over top. Sprinkle with remaining cheese. Cover; bake at 350° for 30 to 35 minutes. Remove cover and bake 5 minutes. Makes 12 servings.

VARIATION: Spread noodles with a small amount of ricotta cheese and sauce. Use all of the Mozzarella cheese for sprinkling on top.

Per serving:

CAL	PRO	CARB	FIB	FAT	SAT	CHOL	SOD
294	10g	31g	<1g	10g	na	43mg	466mg

CHICKEN MEATBALLS

OVEN 400°

Make ahead and keep a supply in the freeze.

1 pound lean ground chicken
1 cup fine fresh bread crumbs
$^1/_2$ cup finely chopped onion
2 egg whites
$^1/_2$ teaspoon salt
$^1/_8$ teaspoon pepper

In medium mixing bowl, combine all the ingredients. Mix until well blended. Form into walnut-size meatballs. Place on baking pan. Bake at 400° for 15 to 18 minutes or until cooked through. Makes 24.

VARIATION: Meat loaf; form into a round loaf in $1^1/_2$-quart shallow baking dish. Bake at 400° for 45 to 50 minutes or until cooked through. Remove from dish; cover and let stand 10 minutes before slicing. (Slices beautifully for meat loaf sandwiches.) Makes 4 servings.

Per meatball:

CAL	PRO	CARB	FIB	FAT	SAT	CHOL	SOD
33	<1g	1g	0g	2g	na	75mg	67mg

FUSILLI CASSEROLE WITH CHICKEN

TOP OF STOVE
OVEN 350°

A family favorite.

6 ounces Fusilli (or other short pasta)
3/4 pound lean ground chicken
1 cup chopped onion
1/3 cup chopped green pepper
2 cups chunky spaghetti sauce
1 cup (4-ounces) Lite Mozzarella cheese, grated

Cook noodles according to package directions. Meanwhile, in large skillet, add chicken, onion, and green pepper. Cook to brown chicken and soften vegetables, stirring frequently. Drain off liquid. Stir in spaghetti sauce. Bring to a boil; reduce heat and simmer 5 minutes. Stir in cheese and pasta. Pour into 2-quart casserole sprayed with vegetable cooking spray. Bake at 350° for 20 minutes. Makes 6 servings.

Per serving:

CAL	PRO	CARB	FIB	FAT	SAT	CHOL	SOD
331	12g	39g	<1g	10g	na	43mg	468mg

CHICKEN CHILI OVER PASTA

TOP OF STOVE

A good everyday dish that makes a lot.

1 pound lean ground chicken
1 cup chopped onion
2 (14 1/2-ounce) cans cut up tomatoes, with juice
2 teaspoons chili powder
4 ounces spaghetti noodles, broken into 3-inch pieces
1 (15-ounce) can light kidney beans, drained

Place ground chicken in large skillet. As chicken starts to brown, add the onion. Continue cooking until chicken is browned and the onion is soft. Stir in tomatoes and chili powder. Bring to a boil, lower heat and simmer about 30 minutes. Meanwhile, cook the spaghetti; drain. Add spaghetti and beans to tomato mixture. Cook until heated through. Makes 6 servins.

Per serving:

CAL	PRO	CARB	FIB	FAT	SAT	CHOL	SOD
287	8g	37g	2g	8g	<1g	50mg	411mg

MEXICAN CHICKEN BAKE

OVEN 400°
TOP OF STOVE

This dish should be eaten on a day when you plan on a no fat, no cholesterol breakfast and lunch.

1 (8½-ounce) package Corn Muffin mix
⅓ cup nonfat milk
¼ cup egg substitute
¾ pound lean ground chicken
1 (8-ounce) package Monterey Jack cheese with jalapéno peppers, shredded
1 (16-ounce) can refried beans

Combine corn muffin mix, milk and egg substitute, mixing just until moistened; batter will be slightly lumpy. Spread in 8x8-inch baking dish sprayed with vegetable cooking spray. Bake at 400° for 12 to 15 minutes or until just cooked through. Do not allow to get too brown. While corn bread is baking, brown chicken in non-stick skillet. Remove from heat; quickly stir in ¾ of the cheese. Spread refried beans evenly over baked corn bread. Top with chicken. Sprinkle remaining cheese on top. Bake at 350° for 15 minutes or until heated through. Cut into squares and serve. Makes 6 servings.

TIP: If you want to add more color to the dish, top each serving with a narrow strip of red pepper for garnish.

Per serving:

CAL	PRO	CARB	FIB	FAT	SAT	CHOL	SOD
482	18g	46g	7g	23g	na	38mg	923mg

Cook's Tip

Thousands of people have been getting sick from the bacteria salmonella in raw eggs. Apparently the inside of the egg an be infected as well as the outer shell. As an extra precaution, it is probably best not to use raw eggs in uncooked recipes, at least until the Poultry Association has done more to solve this problem.

GROUND CHICKEN LOAF

TOP OF STOVE
OVEN 375°

Lower in fat and calories and kind to the budget.

1 pound lean ground chicken
1/2 cup finely chopped onion
1/3 cup finely chopped green pepper
1 1/2 cups soft bread crumbs
2 egg whites
1/4 teaspoon freshly ground pepper

Place chicken in large mixing bowl. Cook onion and green pepper in non-stick skillet sprayed with vegetable cooking spray. If vegetables start to stick add a little water. Cook until soft. Add to ground chicken along with remaining ingredients. Stir gently to mix. Spoon into a 7x5-inch loaf pan. Bake at 375° for 60 minutes or until done. Pour off fat; turn out onto serving dish. Makes 4 servings.

Variation: Serve chicken loaf with catsup or spoon about 1/3 cup catsup over loaf the last 30 minutes of baking time.

Per serving:

CAL	PRO	CARB	FIB	FAT	SAT	CHOL	SOD
217	3g	11g	<1g	11g	na	75g	163g

Salads
Dressings
& Sauces

COMPANY ROMAINE SALAD

8 cups romaine lettuce (bite-size pieces) chilled
1 (6 1/2-ounce) jar marinated artichoke hearts, drained
1/3 cup olive oil
2 tablespoons red wine vinegar
3 tablespoons freshly grated Parmesan cheese, divided
2 medium tomatoes, cut into 16 wedges

Place romaine in large salad bowl. Cut artichokes into small pieces; add to salad. Combine oil, vinegar and 2 tablespoon Parmesan cheese; mix well. Toss salad with just enough dressing to lightly coat leaves. Place on individual salad plates. Sprinkle with remaining Parmesan cheese. Garnish with tomato wedges. Makes 8 servings.

Per serving:

CAL	PRO	CARB	FIB	FAT	SAT	CHOL	SOD
125	3g	4g	2g	11g	2g	2mg	151mg

SALAD WITH ROMAINE

CHILL

1 large bunch romaine lettuce, washed
3 tablespoons olive oil
1 tablespoon apple cider vinegar
1 medium garlic clove, sliced thin
1/2 teaspoon salt
2 small plum tomatoes, sliced

Tear romaine into bite-size pieces. Place in salad bowl; cover and chill until ready to serve. Combine remaining ingredients except tomatoes. Let stand at room temperature about an hour to blend flavors. Remove garlic before serving. Toss romaine with just enough dressing to lightly coat. Garnish with tomato slices. Makes 4 servings.

Per serving:

CAL	PRO	CARB	FIB	FAT	SAT	CHOL	SOD
108	1g	3g	2g	10g	1g	0mg	275mg

TOSSED SALAD WITH ORANGE

A refreshing salad tossed with a light orange dressing.

5 cups assorted salad greens (bite-size pieces)
3 thin slices red onion, separated into rings
1 1/2 medium oranges (seedless)
2 1/2 tablespoons olive oil
1 1/2 teaspoons fresh lemon juice
Salt and pepper to taste

Place greens and onion slices in salad bowl. Peel oranges; cut into thin slices. Take a couple of the slices and squeeze to make 1 1/2 teaspoons juice. Cut remaining slices into quarters; add to salad bowl. Combine orange juice with remaining ingredients; mix well. Toss salad with just enough dressing to lightly coat. Serve. Makes 4 servings.

Per serving:

CAL	PRO	CARB	FIB	FAT	SAT	CHOL	SOD
111	1g	8g	2g	9g	1g	0mg	60mg

SPINACH SALAD

CHILL

A light sweet-sour flavor. Don't plan on any leftovers.

1 large bunch fresh spinach
1/4 cup reduced calorie mayonnaise
1 tablespoon sugar
1 tablespoon white vinegar
1 small red onion, thinly sliced, separated into rings
4 slices lean bacon, cooked, crumbled

Wash spinach thoroughly; let dry. Chill. Meanwhile, combine mayonnaise, sugar and vinegar. Cover; chill to blend flavors. When ready to serve, combine all ingredients with enough dressing to lightly coat leaves. Toss until evenly coated. Serve immediately. Makes 4 servings.

Per serving:

CAL	PRO	CARB	FIB	FAT	SAT	CHOL	SOD
125	4g	9g	3g	8g	2g	10mg	272mg

CASHEW CHICKEN SALAD

CHILL

If ingredients are cut into small pieces, this also makes a nice sandwich filling or use to fill a cantaloupe half.

2 1/2 cups cubed cooked chicken
1/4 cup (1 1/4-ounces) cashews, chopped
1/3 cup thinly sliced celery
2 tablespoons finely chopped mild onion
Salt and pepper to taste
1/3 cup reduced calorie mayonnaise

Combine ingredients, stirring gently to mix. Cover and chill until ready to serve. Makes 4 servings.

TIP: If chilling the salad for more than an hour, you may wish to add the onion just before serving to avoid too strong a flavor.

Per serving:

CAL	PRO	CARB	FIB	FAT	SAT	CHOL	SOD
277	32g	4g	<1g	14g	3g	89mg	413mg

Cook's Tip

Popular vinegars for salads are: White, Red Wine, Herb-Flavored, Sherry, Rice and Fruit Flavored.

MANDARIN CHICKEN SALAD

A complete meal when served with one of your favorite muffins.

2 cooked chicken breast halves, cubed
1 (11-ounce) can Mandarin oranges, drained well
4 1/2 cups shredded lettuce
1/3 cup cashews, split, broken in half
1/4 cup reduced calorie mayonnaise
1 (6-ounce) carton lowfat orange yogurt

In large salad or mixing bowl, combine chicken, oranges, lettuce and cashews. Combine mayonnaise and yogurt. Pour over salad; toss gently to mix. Makes 4 servings.

Per serving:

CAL	PRO	CARB	FIB	FAT	SAT	CHOL	SOD
251	17g	20g	2g	12g	3g	40mg	243mg

Cook's Tip

Margarine

Generally, the softer the margarine the less saturated fat it contains. For instance, liquid squeezable margarine has less saturated fat than soft tub margarine. Soft tub margarine has less saturated fat than soft stick margarine which has less than hard stick margarine.

If you aren't totally confused by now, remember, it is important to read the labels. The first ingredients listed should be a liquid vegetable oil such as safflower, corn, or soybean. Different margarine types are not always interchangable in recipes. It usually isn't advisable to use whipped or diet margarines in most recipes. They usually are incorporated with too much air or water.

CHICKEN PEACH SALAD

CHILL

3 cups cubed cooked chicken
3/4 cup finely chopped celery
2 medium peaches, peeled and cubed
1/4 cup coarsely chopped pecans
1/4 cup honey mustard
1/2 cup reduced calorie mayonnaise

Combine first four ingredients in mixing bowl. Combine mustard and mayonnaise; mix well. Add dressing to salad, tossing to coat. (You may not need all of the dressing.) Cover and chill. Makes 4 servings.

TIP: If fresh peaches aren't in season, use peaches canned in own juice, drained.

Per serving:

CAL	PRO	CARB	FIB	FAT	SAT	CHOL	SOD
258	26g	9g	1g	13g	2g	72mg	318mg

TACO SALAD

TOP OF STOVE

If desired, the meat mixture can be cooked ahead, chilled and reheated.

1 pound extra lean ground beef
1 cup thick 'n chunky salsa
6 cups shredded lettuce
1 cup (4-ounces) reduced fat Cheddar cheese, shredded
1/3 cup sliced ripe olives
1/4 cup Lite sour cream

In medium skillet, brown ground beef. Place in colander to drain off all fat. Return to skillet. Add salsa. Bring to a boil; reduce heat and simmer about 5 minutes or until liquid is absorbed. Arrange lettuce on 4 serving plates. Top each with 1/4 of the meat mixture. Sprinkle with cheese and olives. Top each serving with 1 tablespoon sour cream. Makes 4 servings.

Per serving:

CAL	PRO	CARB	FIB	FAT	SAT	CHOL	SOD
308	32g	7g	2g	18g	9g	96mg	422mg

ORIENTAL PASTA SALAD

TOP OF STOVE
CHILL

5 ounces uncooked rotini noodles
4 ounces fresh Chinese pea pods
1/2 cup thinly sliced carrots
2 tablespoons sugar
1/4 cup olive oil
1 (3-ounce) package Top Ramen Chicken Sesame oriental noodles

Cook rotini noodles according to directions on package. Meanwhile, steam pea pods until just crisp tender. Cut in half crosswise. Drain cooked noodles; rinse. Place noodles in mixing bowl. Add pea pods, carrots, sugar, olive oil and seasoning packet (do not use the sesame oil). Toss thoroughly to blend. Cover; chill 2 hours to blend flavors. When ready to serve, break up 1/2 of the uncooked ramen noodles and add to salad; toss to combine. Makes 8 servings.

Per serving:

CAL	PRO	CARB	FIB	FAT	SAT	CHOL	SOD
172	4g	23g	1g	7g	1g	0mg	42mg

PASTA VEGETABLE SALAD

TOP OF STOVE
CHILL

6 ounces uncooked Fusilli pasta
1 cup raw cauliflower flowerettes
2 cups raw broccoli flowerettes
1 (6-ounce) jar marinated artichoke hearts, drained well
1/2 cup sliced ripe olives
1/4 cup reduced calorie Italian dressing

Cook noodles according to package directions; drain. Place remaining ingredients in large mixing bowl. Add noodles; toss to coat evenly. Cover and chill at least 2 hours before serving. Makes 6 servings.

Per serving:

CAL	PRO	CARB	FIB	FAT	SAT	CHOL	SOD
184	6g	32g	3g	4g	<1g	<1mg	280mg

BROCCOLI-TORTELLINI SALAD

TOP OF STOVE
CHILL

1 (8-ounce) package fresh or frozen cheese tortellini
1 1/2 cups fresh broccoli flowerettes, cooked crisp tender
1/4 cup olive oil
2 tablespoons red wine vinegar
1 tablespoon Dijon mustard
4 plum tomatoes, coarsely chopped

Cook tortellini according to package directions. Meanwhile cook broccoli. Combine oil, vinegar and mustard; mix well. When tortellini is tender, drain and rinse with cold water to cool. Let stand several minutes to drain off the water. In medium bowl, combine tortellini, broccoli and dressing. Cover and chill until ready to serve (at least 1 hour). Add tomatoes. Makes 6 servings.

Per serving:

CAL	PRO	CARB	FIB	FAT	SAT	CHOL	SOD
138	3g	3g	1g	9g	na	na	41mg

EASY COLE SLAW

CHILL

1/2 of a large head cabbage, grated
1 small carrot, grated
1/2 cup reduced calorie mayonnaise
3 tablespoons sugar
2 tablespoons nonfat milk
Salt and pepper to taste

Combine cabbage and carrots in medium bowl. Combine remaining ingredients, adding salt and pepper to taste. Cover and chill until ready to serve. Makes 6 servings.

Per serving:

CAL	PRO	CARB	FIB	FAT	SAT	CHOL	SOD
115	1g	13g	2g	7g	1g	7mg	244mg

Cook's Tip

When purchasing packaged noodles, read labels carefully and avoid those made with eggs.

MARINATED VEGETABLE SALAD

TOP OF STOVE
CHILL

2 cups sliced carrots, about 1/4-inch thick
1 medium onion, sliced, separated into rings
4 ounces fresh Chinese pea pods
2 tablespoons olive oil
2 tablespoons sugar
1 (3-ounce) package Top Ramen Chicken Sesame oriental noodles

Place carrots and onion in large steamer basket. Cover; cook over boiling water 3 to 4 minutes. Place in mixing bowl. Add peas to steamer basket; cook until vegetables are just crisp tender. Combine oil, sugar and dry seasoning packet with 1 tablespoon water (do not use the sesame oil). Pour over vegetables; toss to coat. Cover; chill at least 2 hours before serving. Makes 3 cups.

OPTIONAL: Just before serving, toss with 1/4 of the dry noodles, crumbled.

Per 1/2 cup serving;

CAL	PRO	CARB	FIB	FAT	SAT	CHOL	SOD
110	2g	15g	3g	5g	<1g	0mg	67mg

COOL CUCUMBER SALAD

TOP OF STOVE
CHILL

Nice as a side dish or added to a tossed green salad. Will keep for several days.

2 large or 3 medium cucumbers, 3 1/2 cups, peeled and sliced thin
1 medium mild onion, sliced, separated into rings
1 small red or green pepper, thinly sliced
1/2 teaspoon celery seed
1 cup sugar
1/2 cup apple cider vinegar

Place vegetables and celery seed in large mixing bowl. Combine sugar and vinegar in small saucepan. Bring to a boil; cook just until sugar is dissolved. Pour over cucumber mixture; toss to coat. Let stand at least 2 hours, stirring frequently. Chill until ready to serve. Drain before serving. Makes about 5 cups.

Per 1/2 cup serving:

CAL	PRO	CARB	FIB	FAT	SAT	CHOL	SOD
99	<1g	25g	1g	<1g	0g	0mg	3mg

FRESH FRUIT SALAD IN CANTALOUPE
Serve as a refreshing salad or a light dessert.

> 2 small cantaloupes, halved
> 1 cup sliced strawberries
> 1 cup sliced nectarines
> 1 cup cubed pineapple
> $^1/_3$ cup blueberries
> $^1/_2$ cup sliced kiwi

Remove seeds from cantaloupe. Place on serving dishes. Combine fruit; fill cantaloupes. Makes 4 servings.

VARIATION: Omit cantaloupe halves. Add 1 cup cubed cantaloupe to above mixture; toss and serve.

Per serving:

Cal	Pro	Carb	Fib	Fat	Sat	Chol	Sod
159	3g	38g	5g	1g	<1g	0mg	26mg

ORANGE FRUIT SALAD CHILL
A favorite with children.

> 1 (11-ounce) can Mandarin oranges, drained
> 1 (16-ounce) can pineapple tidbits, drained
> 3 large bananas, sliced
> 1 (8-ounce) container Lite frozen whipped topping, thawed
> 1 (3-ounce) package orange jello

In large mixing bowl, combine oranges, pineapple and banana. Combine whipped topping with the jello, stirring until dissolved and blended. Fold into fruit. Chill at least 2 hours. Makes 12 servings.

Per serving:

Cal Sod	Pro	Carb	Fib	Fat		Sat	Chol
126	3g	25g	1g	5g	0g	0mg	14mg

JELLO FRUIT SALAD

CHILL

1 (6-ounce) package strawberry jello
1 cup thinly sliced peaches
1 cup sliced strawberries
1 cup sliced bananas

Combine jello with 2 cups boiling water; stir until dissolved. Add 2 cups cold water. Chill until consistency of unbeaten egg white. Fold in fruit. Pour into 9 x 13-inch baking dish. Chill until set. Makes 15 servings.

Per serving:

CAL	PRO	CARB	FIB	FAT	SAT	CHOL	SOD
59	4g	11g	<1g	<1g	0g	0mg	21mg

PINEAPPLE JELLO SALAD

CHILL

A light fluffy cooling type of salad.

1 (3-ounce) package lemon jello
1/2 cup nonfat plain yogurt
1 large banana, sliced
1 (8-ounce) can crushed pineapple, drained thoroughly

Combine jello with 1 cup boiling water; stir to dissolve completely. Add 1/2 cup cold water. Chill until slightly thickened; this may take up to an hour or so. In mixer bowl, combine jello and yogurt; beat until fluffy. Stir in bananas and pineapple. Pour into 8 x 8-inch baking dish. Cover and chill until set. This sets up rather quickly. Makes 9 servings.

Per serving:

CAL	PRO	CARB	FIB	FAT	SAT	CHOL	SOD
72	5g	14g	<1g	<1g	0g	<1mg	26mg

GARLIC MUSTARD VINAIGRETTE

A good stand-by and better than store bought.

2 tablespoons garlic red wine vinegar
5 tablespoons olive oil
1 1/2 teaspoons Dijon mustard
3/4 teaspoon salt
1/8 teaspoon freshly ground black pepper

Combine ingredients in small container, stirring to blend. Cover tightly and shake vigorously to mix well. If not using right away, store in refrigerator. Makes about 1/2 cup.

Per tablespoon:

CAL	PRO	CARB	FIB	FAT	SAT	CHOL	SOD
76	0g	<1g	0g	8g	1g	0mg	212mg

VERSATILE VINAIGRETTE

This dressing is very good served over almost any green salad as well as many pasta salads. Low in sodium.

1/4 cup olive oil
2 tablespoons red wine vinegar
1 tablespoon Dijon mustard

Combine ingredients; mix well to blend. Makes almost 1/2 cup.

Per tablespoon:

CAL	PRO	CARB	FIB	FAT	SAT	CHOL	SOD
71	<1g	<1g	0g	8g	1g	0mg	28mg

SWEET-SOUR GARLIC DRESSING

Since this makes a small amount of dressing there is less waste. Goes with almost any combination of salad greens. Very low in sodium.

3 tablespoons garlic red wine vinegar
2 tablespoons olive oil
2 tablespoons sugar
1 small garlic clove, minced

Combine ingredients; mix well. Let stand at least 30 minutes or overnight (in refrigerator) to blend flavors. Makes 1/3 cup.

Per tablespoon:

CAL	PRO	CARB	FIB	FAT	SAT	CHOL	SOD
49	0g	4g	0g	4g	<1g	0mg	<1mg

DIETER'S SALAD DRESSING

CHILL

This is great for a no-fat dressing. If desired, add 2 tablespoons finely chopped onion.

1/4 cup red wine vinegar
1/4 cup fresh lemon juice
6 small packets sugar substitute (or to taste)
1/2 teaspoon dry mustard
1/2 teaspoon salt
1/4 teaspoon freshly ground black pepper

Combine ingredients in small jar. Cover; chill to blend flavors. Makes 1/2 cup.

Per tablespoon:

CAL	PRO	CARB	FIB	FAT	SAT	CHOL	SOD
6	0g	2g	0g	<1g	0g	0mg	158mg

Cook's Tip

Try to use low-fat dressings for everyday use and save the higher fat dressings for special occasions or eating out.

PINEAPPLE DRESSING

CHILL

A nice tart-sweet dressing to serve over fresh fruit or spinach salad.

6 tablespoons Canola oil
7 tablespoons pineapple juice
3 1/2 tablespoons red wine vinegar
2 tablespoons honey
1 teaspoon poppy seeds

Combine ingredients in small container; mix well. Cover; refrigerate to blend flavors. Makes 1 cup.

Per tablespoon:

CAL	PRO	CARB	FIB	FAT	SAT	CHOL	SOD
58	0g	3g	0g	5g	<1g	0mg	<1mg

POPPY SEED DRESSING

My favorite! Serve over spinach salad or fresh fruit.

1/3 cup honey
1/3 cup white wine vinegar
2 teaspoons Dijon mustard
3 tablespoons chopped onion
1 cup Canola oil
1 tablespoon poppy seeds

Place first 4 ingredients in blender or food processor; mix until smooth. Gradually add oil and blend until mixture thickens. Stir in poppy seeds. Store in refrigerator. Will keep several days. Makes 1 1/2 cups.

Per tablespoon:

CAL	PRO	CARB	FIB	FAT	SAT	CHOL	SOD
98	<1g	4g	0g	9g	<1g	0mg	6mg

YOGURT-FRUIT DRESSING

Serve over a fresh fruit salad or a combination of canned and fresh fruit.

1 (8-ounce) container lowfat raspberry yogurt
3/4 cup Lite frozen whipped topping, thawed

Combine ingredients, mixing to blend well. Serve over fresh fruit or serve as a dip. Makes 1 1/2 cups.

Per tablespoon:

CAL	PRO	CARB	FIB	FAT	SAT	CHOL	SOD
14	<1g	2g	0g	<1g	na	<1g	6mg

LEMON MAYONNAISE DRESSING

CHILL

This is wonderful on a salad of romaine lettuce, raw mushrooms, crisp croutons and a sprinkle of grated Parmesan cheese.

1/4 cup mayonnaise (for best flavor, do not use reduced calorie)
1/4 cup Lite sour cream
1 teaspoon lemon juice
1 1/2 teaspoons Dijon mustard
1/2 teaspoon dried dill weed
Dash garlic powder

Combine ingredients and mix thoroughly. Cover and chill to blend flavors. Makes 1/2 cup.

TIP: Splurge on this recipe and use your favorite mayonnaise (not reduced calorie or light). Depending on the brand of sour cream you use, you may wish to stir in a small amount of skim milk for desired consistency.

Per tablespoon:

CAL	PRO	CARB	FIB	FAT	SAT	CHOL	SOD
61	<1g	<1g	0g	6g	1g	7mg	56mg

BARBECUE SAUCE

TOP OF STOVE

A sauce with a kick - nice and spicy. Excellent on chicken.

1/2 cup finely chopped onion
1 (8-ounce) can tomato sauce
3 tablespoons firmly packed light brown sugar
2 teaspoons chili powder
1/3 cup cider vinegar
1/8 teaspoon Tabasco

Combine ingredients in small saucepan. Bring to a boil; reduce heat and simmer 5 to 6 minutes or until onion is tender. Makes 1 1/4 cups.

TIP: This sauce works best on chicken pieces that have the skin removed. If baking in oven, brush some of the sauce on chicken, bake 45 to 60 minutes, brushing frequently with the sauce (chicken breasts will take less time to cook than the dark meat). If grilling, brush sauce on chicken last 20 minutes of cooking time.

Per tablespoon:

CAL	PRO	CARB	FIB	FAT	SAT	CHOL	SOD
15	<1g	4g	<1g	<1g	0g	0mg	6mg

BBQ SAUCE

This is enough sauce for one pound turkey meatballs, one chicken cut up or four chicken breast halves.

3/4 cup barbecue sauce
3/4 teaspoon Worcestershire sauce
1 tablespoon firmly packed light brown sugar
1 tablespoon catsup

Combine ingredients; mix well. Makes 3/4 cup sauce.

TIP: There are many different kinds of barbecue sauces on the market and each has its own unique flavor which affects the end result of a recipe. For this sauce I used Hunt's Thick and Rich barbecue sauce. If using meatballs (cooked), pour sauce over top and bake at 350° for 30 minutes or until heated through.

Per tablespoon:

CAL	PRO	CARB	FIB	FAT	SAT	CHOL	SOD
17	<1g	3g	<1g	<1g	0g	0mg	143mg

CHERRY SAUCE FOR HAM

TOP OF STOVE

Easy! Can be made ahead.

1 (16-ounce) can tart red cherries, save juice
1/4 cup sugar
1 tablespoon cornstarch
1/8 teaspoon almond extract

Drain juice from cherries; you should have about 1/2 cup. In small saucepan, combine sugar and cornstarch. Gradually stir in the juice. Add extract. Cook over medium low heat, stirring frequently, until slightly thickened. Add cherries; cook until heated through. Makes 2 cups.

TIP: If you find this a little too tart for your taste, add a small amount of sugar.

Per tablespoon:

CAL	PRO	CARB	FIB	FAT	SAT	CHOL	SOD
11	0g	3g	<1g	<1g	0g	0mg	<1mg

CRANBERRY CHILI SAUCE

TOP OF STOVE

This sweet-tart sauce can be used with meatballs and served as an appetizer or a main course.

1 (16-ounce) can cranberry sauce
1 (12-ounce) bottle chili sauce
1 teaspoon lemon juice
1 teaspoon grated lemon peel
2 tablespoons firmly packed light brown sugar

Combine ingredients in medium saucepan. Stir to blend thoroughly. Bring to a boil; reduce heat and simmer 3 to 4 minutes. Makes about 3 cups.

TIP: This is enough sauce for 2 recipes of Turkey Meatballs (page 154). If using cooked meatballs, add to sauce and heat through. Make small meatballs for appetizers and larger meatballs for a main course.

Per tablespoon of sauce:

CAL	PRO	CARB	FIB	FAT	SAT	CHOL	SOD
24	<1g	5g	<1g	<1g	<1g	0mg	98mg

CRANBERRY-APPLE RELISH

TOP OF STOVE
CHILL

A nice accompaniment to pork, ham or chicken.

1 cup raw cranberries, fresh or frozen
1 cup chopped Rome apples
2/3 cup sugar
1/4 teaspoon powdered ginger
2 tablespoons orange juice

Combine ingredients in medium saucepan; stir to blend. Bring to a boil; reduce heat and simmer about 15 minutes or until cranberries burst and apples are cooked through (there will be some liquid remaining in pan, but mixture will thicken as it cools). Cool; store in refrigerator until ready to serve. Makes 1 cup.

Per tablespoon:

CAL	PRO	CARB	FIB	FAT	SAT	CHOL	SOD
40	0g	10g	<1g	<1g	0g	0mg	<1mg

MUSHROOM SAUCE

TOP OF STOVE

A very low fat spaghetti sauce.

1/2 pound fresh mushrooms, sliced
1 cup coarsely chopped onion
1 teaspoon soft tub margarine
2 (8-ounce) cans tomato sauce
1 teaspoon Italian herbs

Over medium heat, cook mushrooms and onion in margarine in medium non-stick skillet until cooked through. Stir in tomato sauce and herbs. Bring to a boil, reduce heat, and simmer covered, about 15 minutes to blend flavors. Makes 4 servings.

Per serving:

CAL	PRO	CARB	FIB	FAT	SAT	CHOL	SOD
79	3g	16g	4g	1g	<1g	0mg	37mg

MARINADE

An excellent marinade for beef, meat kabobs and poultry.

1/4 cup reduced sodium soy sauce, plus 2 tablespoons
1/4 cup firmly packed light brown sugar, plus 2 tablespoons
2 tablespoons white vinegar
1 tablespoon, plus 1 1/2 teaspoons Worcestershire sauce
1 teaspoon Canola oil
2 to 3 slices fresh ginger (or 1/2 teaspoon ground ginger)

Combine ingredients; mix well to dissolve sugar. Pour over choice of meat and marinade at least 2 hours or overnight.

NOTE: We have not included the analysis of this recipe because the amount of marinade absorbed into the meat, per serving, is neglible.

EASY BORDELAISE SAUCE

TOP OF STOVE

Serve with beef tenderloin and steaks.

1/4 cup finely chopped onion
3 tablespoons soft tub margarine, divided
1/2 teaspoon finely crumbled bay leaves
1 cup red Burgundy wine
5 teaspoons cornstarch
1 (10 1/2-ounce) can beef broth concentrate (do not dilute)

In small saucepan, sauté onion in 2 tablespoons of the margarine, cooking until soft, but not brown. Add bay leaves and wine. Simmer until reduced to about one-third of its original volume. Combine cornstarch with 1/4 cup of the broth; mix until smooth. Stir into wine mixture along with remaining broth. Cook until thickened, stirring frequently. Add remaining 1 tablespoon margarine. Makes about 1 3/4 cups.

Per tablespoon:

CAL	PRO	CARB	FIB	FAT	SAT	CHOL	SOD
21	<1g	1g	0g	1g	<1g	0mg	80mg

PINEAPPLE PEPPER SAUCE

TOP OF STOVE

This is a nice sweet-sour sauce to serve over rice. Also delicious when you add 1 recipe Turkey Meatballs, page 154, and serve as a main course over rice or as appetizers.

2 (8-ounce) cans pineapple chunks (save 1 tablespoon juice)
1/2 cup grape jelly
1 (12-ounce) bottle chili sauce
2 tablespoons apple cider vinegar
1 medium large green pepper, cut into small squares
1 medium large red pepper, cut into small squares

In large saucepan, combine pineapple, the 1 tablespoon juice, jelly, chilli sauce and vinegar. Cook over medium heat, stirring frequently. When mixture starts to boil, reduce heat and simmer about 5 minutes. Add peppers; cook about 5 minutes more or until peppers are tender, but not soft. (If you are adding cooked meatballs, add with the peppers). Makes 4 servings as a main course.

Per serving:

CAL	PRO	CARB	FIB	FAT	SAT	CHOL	SOD
284	3g	72g	3g	<1g	0g	0mg	
1149mg							

ONION AND MUSHROOM TOPPING

TOP OF STOVE

A nice topping for hamburgers, turkeyburgers and meatloaf.

1 large onion, thinly sliced and separated into rings
1 cup sliced fresh mushrooms
1 teaspoon soft tub margarine
1/2 teaspoon Worcestershire sauce

Cook onion and mushrooms in margarine in medium non-stick skillet sprayed wtih vegetable cooking spray, stirring frequently, until just tender. Add Worcestershire sauce and 1 tablespoon water; stir to blend. Makes 4 servings.

Per serving:

CAL	PRO	CARB	FIB	FAT	SAT	CHOL	SOD
46	2g	8g	2g	1g<1g	0mg	11mg	

PIZZA SAUCE

TOP OF STOVE

It takes only minutes to make your own pizza sauce.

2 (8-ounce) cans tomato sauce
2 teaspoons Italian herbs
1 tablespoon freshly grated Parmesan cheese

Combine tomato sauce, herbs and Parmesan in medium saucepan; mix well. Bring to a boil, reduce heat, and simmer 15 to 20 minutes or until thickened. Let cool before using or store in refrigerator. Makes about 1 1/4 cups.

16-inch pizza	**1 1/4 cups sauce**
14-inch pizza	**1 cup sauce**
12-inch pizza	**3/4 cup sauce**

Per 1/4 cup:

CAL	PRO	CARB	FIB	FAT	SAT	CHOL	SOD
33	2g	7g	1g	<1g	<1g	1mg	44mg

QUICK SPAGHETTI SAUCE

TOP OF STOVE

If short on time, you will enjoy the simplicity of this recipe.

1 (14 1/2-ounce) can chunky stewed tomatoes, with juice
1 (6-ounce) can tomato paste
1 teaspoon sugar
1/4 teaspoon oregano
1 (2-ounce) can mushroom slices or stems (or use fresh)
1/2 cup water

Combine all the ingredients in a medium saucepan; bring to a boil. Reduce heat and simmer 10 minutes. Makes 3 cups.

TIP: This sauce can be substituted for the purchased spaghetti sauce in the recipe Onion Spaghetti Dinner on page 209.

Per 1/2 cup serving:

CAL	PRO	CARB	FIB	FAT	SAT	CHOL	SOD
45	2g	11g	2g	<1g	0g	0mg	420mg

SAUERBRATEN SAUCE

TOP OF STOVE

Another excellent sauce that goes well with meatballs.

3/4 cup pineapple juice
1 teaspoon beef bouillon granules
3 tablespoons firmly packed light brown sugar
2 teaspoons lemon juice
1/4 cup raisins
1/3 cup (about 4) gingersnap cookies, coarsely crushed

In medium saucepan, combine juice, bouillon granules, brown sugar and lemon juice with 3/4 cup water. Bring to a boil; stir in raisins and crushed cookies. Continue to cook, about 3 to 4 minutes. Makes about **1 3/4** cups.

TIP: Meatballs can be added frozen, thawed or just baked. Cook 15 to 20 minutes to thicken sauce and to heat meatballs.

Per tablespoon:

CAL	PRO	CARB	FIB	FAT	SAT	CHOL	SOD
16	<1g	4g	<1g	<1g	0g	0mg	41mg

STROGANOFF SAUCE

TOP OF STOVE

Just add Turkey Meatballs, page 154, or 1 1/4 pounds browned ground chicken to this quick and easy sauce.

2 teaspoons soft tub margarine
1 cup finely chopped onion
1/4 cup flour
2 cups chicken broth
1 cup Lite sour cream
Salt and pepper to taste

Melt margarine in large non-stick skillet. Add onion; cook until soft, stirring frequently to prevent browning. Add flour. Stir until onion is coated thoroughly with the flour. Gradually stir in broth, mixing well to blend. Cook, stirring frequently, until thickened. Stir in sour cream. Cook until heated through, but do not boil. Add salt and pepper to taste.

Per 1/2 cup serving:

CAL	PRO	CARB	FIB	FAT	SAT	CHOL	SOD
82	4g	8g	<1g	5g	2g	12mg	343mg

SWEET AND SOUR SAUCE

TOP OF STOVE

Serve with chicken nuggets. Can make ahead and reheat.

1/2 cup sugar
1/4 cup white vinegar
2 tablespoons catsup
1/2 cup water, divided
1 tablespoon cornstarch, plus 1 teaspoon

In small saucepan, combine sugar, vinegar, catsup and 6 tablespoons of the water. Bring to a boil. Combine cornstarch with remaining 2 tablespoons water; add to sauce. Cook, stirring frequently, until thickened and smooth. Makes 1 cup.

Per tablespoon:

CAL	PRO	CARB	FIB	FAT	SAT	CHOL	SOD
29	0g	8g	0g	0g	0g	0mg	23mg

Cook's Tip

Avoid:

The following oils are very high in saturated fat and should be avoided:

Coconut oil
Palm oil
Palm kernel oil

Read labels carefully.

PINEAPPLE CRANBERRY SAUCE

TOP OF STOVE

Add meatballs, cooked cubed chicken or pork, or tiny sausages. Serve as an appetizer with toothpicks or over rice as a main dish.

1/2 cup barbecue sauce
1 cup jellied cranberry sauce
1 (8-ounce) can crushed pineapple, with juice

Combine ingredients in medium saucepan, stirring to mix. Cook over low heat until blended. Bring to a boil; reduce heat. (At this point add your choice of meat; simmer until heated through.) Makes 2 cups sauce.

Per 1/4 serving, sauce only:

CAL	PRO	CARB	FIB	FAT	SAT	CHOL	SOD
81	<1g	20g	1g	<1g	0g	0mg	138mg

MILK GRAVY

TOP OF STOVE

You won't get any complaints with this recipe. Very good over hot biscuits or mashed potatoes.

1/4 cup nonfat powdered milk
2 tablespoons cornstarch, plus 2 teaspoons
2 cups chicken broth
1/2 teaspoon salt
1/8 teaspoon freshly ground black pepper

In medium saucepan, combine powdered milk and cornstarch. Stir in broth until smooth. Cook over medium heat until mixture thickens, stirring frequently with a whisk. Add salt and pepper. Makes about 1 3/4 cups.

TIP: If you need to reduce your sodium intake, omit the salt. If using canned broth, it does contain sodium which may be enough for your taste.

Per tablespoon:

CAL	PRO	CARB	FIB	FAT	SAT	CHOL	SOD
7	<1g	1g	0g	<1g	0g	<1mg	113mg

MOCK SOUR CREAM-CREAM CHEESE

CHILL

Can be used in some recipes as a substitute for sour cream or cream cheese. You may have to do some experimenting.

2 cups nonfat plain yogurt (cannot contain gelatin)

Place a large bowl-shaped type of coffee filter in a colander. Place colander in a larger bowl. Add yogurt. Cover and refrigerate 8 to 10 hours or until all liquid has drained off. Discard liquid. Makes about 1 cup.

Per tablespoon:

CAL	PRO	CARB	FIB	FAT	SAT	CHOL	SOD
8	<1g	1g	0g	<1g	0g	<1mg	11mg

LEMON SAUCE

TOP OF STOVE

Serve warm over Angel Food Cake, Sponge Cake or gingerbread.

2 tablespoons, plus 1 teaspoon cornstarch
1/2 cup sugar
1 cup water
1 lemon (2 teaspoons grated peel and 2 tablespoons juice)
1 tablespoon soft tub margarine

Combine cornstarch and sugar in medium saucepan. Stir in water. Cook over medium heat, stirring frequently, until thickened. Add lemon peel, lemon juice and margarine. Cook until heated through. Makes 1 1/4 cups sauce.

TIP: Sauce will thicken as it cools. Reheats nicely in microwave.

Per serving:

CAL	PRO	CARB	FIB	FAT	SAT	CHOL	SOD
18	0g	2g	0g	1g	<1g	0mg	10mg

MANDARIN ORANGE SAUCE

TOP OF STOVE

A "simply delicious" sauce served over Angel Food cake, frozen yogurt or ice milk.

1 (11-ounce) can Mandarin oranges with juice
2 teaspoons cornstarch
3 tablespoons orange marmalade

Drain juice from oranges into small saucepan. Stir in cornstarch until blended. Add marmalade. Cook over medium heat, stirring frequently, until sauce thickens. Add orange segments. Remove from heat. Let cool; serve at room temperature. Makes 1 1/2 cups.

Per 1/4 cup serving:

CAL	PRO	CARB	FIB	FAT	SAT	CHOL	SOD
49	<1g	13g	<1g	0g	0g	0mg	5mg

CHOCOLATE SAUCE

TOP OF STOVE
CHILL

Cocoa powder and Canola oil are substitutes for chocolate squares and skim milk replaces whole milk in this popular recipe.

3/4 cup cocoa powder
4 tablespoons Canola oil
3 cups sugar
1 (12-ounce) can evaporated skim milk
1 teaspoon vanilla extract

In top of double boiler, thoroughly combine cocoa and oil. Heat mixture over boiling water. Gradually stir in sugar; add some of the milk if mixture is too thick. When combined, stir in remaining milk and vanilla. Pour into jar and store covered in refrigerator for several hours or overnight. Makes 4 cups.

Per tablespoon:

CAL	PRO	CARB	FIB	FAT	SAT	CHOL	SOD
50	<1g	10g	<1g	1g	<1g	<1mg	13mg

BLUEBERRY SAUCE

TOP OF STOVE

Very good served over Angel Food cake, lemon mousse and cheesecake.

1 cup sugar
1 1/2 tablespoons cornstarch
1 teaspoon freshly grated lemon peel
1 cup water
3 cups fresh or frozen blueberries (partially thawed, if frozen)

In medium saucepan, mix sugar, cornstarch and lemon peel. Gradually stir in water; mixing to thoroughly blend. Cook over medium-low heat until thickened, stirring frequently. Add blueberries. Bring to a boil; remove from heat. Cover and chill until ready to serve. Makes 4 cups.

Per tablespoon:

CAL	PRO	CARB	FIB	FAT	SAT	CHOL	SOD
17	<1g	4g	<1g	<1g	0g	0mg	<1mg

CHERRY CINNAMON TOPPING

TOP OF STOVE

Wonderful served warm or cold over vanilla ice milk or Orange Cheesecake Pie, page 63.

1 (17-ounce) can dark sweet cherries, pitted, save juice
2 tablespoons sugar
1 tablespoon cornstarch
1/4 teaspoon cinnamon
3 long strips peel from an orange

Drain cherries saving juice, there should be about 1 cup. In small saucepan, combine sugar, cornstarch and cinnamon. Gradually stir in juice; mix well. Add orange peel. Cook over low heat until thickened, stirring frequently. Add cherries and heat through. Serve warm or cold. Makes about 2 cups.

Per tablespoon:

CAL	PRO	CARB	FIB	FAT	SAT	CHOL	SOD
13	<1g	3g	<1g	<1g	0g	0mg	0mg

Vegetables

ASPARAGUS TOMATO STIR-FRY

TOP OF STOVE

1 pound fresh asparagus
1 small onion, cut into narrow wedges, separated
2 teaspoons reduced sodium soy sauce
1/8 teaspoon ground ginger
1/2 teaspoon cornstarch
10 cherry tomatoes, halved

Wash asparagus; snap off ends and cut into 1 1/2-inch slices. Place asparagus and onion in large heavy skillet. Add 4 tablespoons water. Place over medium high heat; cover and cook 5 to 7 minutes or until vegetables are just crisp tender, adding more water if needed. In small bowl, combine soy sauce, ginger and cornstarch; mix until smooth. Stir into vegetables; add tomatoes. Cook, stirring occasionally until heated through. Makes 4 servings.

Per serving:

CAL	PRO	CARB	FIB	FAT	SAT	CHOL	SOD
70	4g	13g	3g	<1g	<1g	0mg	92mg

ASPARAGUS WITH ALMONDS

TOP OF STOVE

2 pounds fresh asparagus
1 tablespoon soft tub margarine, divided
1 tablespoon slivered almonds
1 (8-ounce) can sliced water chestnuts

Clean asparagus; snap off ends. Slice diagonally into 1 1/2-inch pieces. Place in medium skillet. Add 1/4 cup water. Cover; steam over medium heat until crisp tender. Time will vary according to thickness of asparagus but it doesn't take more than a few minutes. Drain off water. Remove asparagus and keep warm. Melt 1 1/2 teaspoons of the margarine in skillet. Add almonds and toast until light golden. Add water chestnuts; heat through. Add asparagus and remaining margarine. Toss gently to mix and heat through. Makes 4 servings.

Per serving:

CAL	PRO	CARB	FIB	FAT	SAT	CHOL	SOD
119	7g	17g	5g	5g	<1g	0mg	37mg

Fresh Asparagus with Red Peppers

Top of Stove

A colorful fresh vegetable dish.

1 1/4 pounds fresh asparagus spears
1/2 small red pepper, cut into narrow strips
1 teaspoon soft tub margarine
Dash of freshly ground black pepper
1 teaspoon freshly grated Parmesan cheese

Wash asparagus; snap off ends where they break easily. Place asparagus and pepper strips in steamer basket. Cover; steam over hot water, 5 to 7 minutes or until just crisp tender. Place in serving dish. Gently toss with margarine. Sprinkle with pepper and Parmesan. Makes 4 servings.

Per serving:

Cal	Pro	Carb	Fib	Fat	Sat	Chol	Sod
48	4g	7g	3g	1g	<1g	<1mg	19mg

Pasta with Artichoke Tomato Sauce

Top of Stove

A quick meatless dish you can prepare in 30 minutes. Serve with a hearty tossed green salad and Italian bread.

1 (6-ounce) jar marinated artichoke hearts
2 medium garlic cloves, minced
1 (28-ounce) can whole tomatoes, drained and coarsely chopped
1/8 teaspoon freshly ground black pepper
8 ounces uncooked mostaccioli noodles
4 teaspoons grated Parmesan cheese

Put water on to boil for the pasta. Cook noodles according to directions on package; drain. Meanwhile drain artichokes, reserving 1 tablespoon of the marinade. Thinly slice artichokes crosswise, discarding any tough outer leaves. In medium skillet, heat the reserved marinade. Add garlic and quickly sauté until soft, but not browned. Add chopped tomatoes, artichokes and pepper. Bring to a boil; reduce heat and simmer 15 to 20 minutes. Place noodles on large serving platter. Top with sauce; sprinkle with Parmesan. Makes 4 large servings.

Per serving:

Cal	Pro	Carb	Fib	Fat	Sat	Chol	Sod
337	12g	63g	4g	5g	<1g	1mg	498mg

GREEN BEANS DIJON

TOP OF STOVE

2 teaspoons soft tub margarine
1 tablespoon chopped almonds
1½ teaspoons lemon juice
1 teaspoon Dijon mustard
1 (16-ounce) can green beans, heated, drained (or ½ pound cooked fresh beans)

Heat margarine in small skillet. Add almonds and toast lightly. Stir in lemon juice and mustard. Pour mixture over hot beans and toss gently to coat. Makes 4 servings.

Per serving:

CAL	PRO	CARB	FIB	FAT	SAT	CHOL	SOD
50	2g	5g	2g	3g	<1g	0mg	281mg

GREEN BEAN MEDLEY

TOP OF STOVE

A full-flavor green bean dish using just a small amount of margarine.

⅓ cup finely chopped onion
1 teaspoon soft tub margarine
2 strips bacon, cooked and crumbled
1 (16-ounce) can green beans, drained
Salt and pepper to taste

Cook onion in margarine, in non-stick skillet, until soft. Add bacon and green beans. Salt and pepper to taste. Cook until heated through. Makes 4 servings.

Per serving:

CAL	PRO	CARB	FIB	FAT	SAT	CHOL	SOD
67	3g	9g	2g	3g	<1g	3mg	362mg

EASY BAKED BEANS

OVEN 350°

Delicious served hot or cold.

1 (31-ounce) can pork and beans
1/3 cup firmly packed light brown sugar
1/3 cup finely chopped onion
1/2 cup catsup
1 teaspoon prepared mustard
1 (8-ounce) can crushed pineapple, drained

Combine ingredients in 2-quart casserole sprayed with vegetable cooking spray; mix well. Bake at 350° (325° if using glass) for 60 to 75 minutes, stirring a couple of times. Beans should be slightly thickened but not dry. They will thicken as they stand. Makes 6 servings.

Per serving:

CAL	PRO	CARB	FIB	FAT	SAT	CHOL	SOD
254	8g	55g	9g	2g	<1g	10mg	749mg

BROCCOLI-TOMATO DISH

TOP OF STOVE
OVEN 350°

Has both eye and taste appeal.

4 cups fresh broccoli flowerettes, bite-size pieces
1 teaspoon soft tub margarine, melted
1/4 teaspoon oregano
Salt and pepper to taste
2 medium tomatoes, cut into 16 wedges
1/3 cup (1 1/2-ounces) Lite Mozzarella cheese, shredded

Cook broccoli until just crisp tender. Toss lightly with margarine, oregano, salt and pepper. Place in 10-inch oven proof serving dish. Arrange tomato wedges around edge. Sprinkle with cheese. Bake at 350° about 5 minutes or until tomatoes are heated through and cheese is melted. Makes 4 servings.

Per serving:

CAL	PRO	CARB	FIB	FAT	SAT	CHOL	SOD
75	8g	8g	4g	2g	1g	3mg	155mg

FRESH BROCCOLI WITH GARLIC

MICROWAVE
TOP OF STOVE

1 bunch broccoli, about 1¼ pounds
1 tablespoon olive oil
2 large garlic cloves, minced
2 tablespoons chicken broth
Salt and pepper to taste

Cut broccoli stems about 1½ inches below the flowerettes; separate into serving pieces. Place in a medium size bowl; add about ¼ cup water. Cover; microwave on high, about 4 minutes or until broccoli is just crisp tender. Remove from microwave; drain. Meanwhile, heat oil in medium non-stick skillet. Add garlic; sauté about 2 minutes. Add broth; bring to a boil. Add broccoli; toss gently and heat through. Drain off liquid. Season to taste with salt and pepper. Makes 4 servings.

Per serving:

CAL	PRO	CARB	FIB	FAT	SAT	CHOL	SOD
72	4g	8g	4g	4g	<1g	0mg	53mg

SWEET-SOUR BRUSSELS SPROUTS

TOP OF STOVE

Even if you aren't too fond of Brussels sprouts, you might enjoy this sweet-sour version.

1 pound fresh Brussels sprouts
1 teaspoon Canola oil
½ cup finely chopped onion
¼ cup cider vinegar
2 tablespoons sugar
¼ teaspoon dry mustard

Wash and trim Brussels sprouts. Place oil in medium non-stick skillet. Add onion. Combine remaining ingredients; add to skillet. Add Brussels sprouts; stir to coat. Bring to a boil; reduce heat, cover and simmer 10 to 12 minutes or until crisp tender. Makes 4 servings.

VARIATION: For a special dinner, I like to sprinkle the cooked Brussels sprouts with 2 strips of cooked and crumbled bacon.

Per serving:

CAL	PRO	CARB	FIB	FAT	SAT	CHOL	SOD
88	3g	19g	5g	2g	<1g	0mg	29mg

CANDIED CARROTS

TOP OF STOVE

A recipe you will want to make often.

1 pound carrots, cut julienne style
2 teaspoons soft tub margarine
2 tablespoons firmly packed light brown sugar
1/4 teaspoon salt (optional)
1/4 teaspoon cracked pepper

Place carrots in medium saucepan. Add about 1/4-inch water. Cover; bring to a boil and cook 3 to 4 minutes. Drain off water. Add margarine, brown sugar, salt and pepper; stir to coat. Continue cooking until carrots are just crisp tender. Makes 4 servings.

Per serving (without salt):

CAL	PRO	CARB	FIB	FAT	SAT	CHOL	SOD
94	1g	19g	4g	2g	<1g	0mg	93mg

CARROTS AND PEA PODS

TOP OF STOVE

4 large carrots, 2 1/2 cups
1 cup (4-ounces) fresh pea pods
1 teaspoon soft tub margarine
Salt and pepper to taste

Cut carrots into 1/2-inch diagonal slices. Place in medium saucepan along with about 1/4 cup water. Bring to a boil; cover and cook 3 to 4 minutes. Add pea pods. Cover; cook 4 to 5 minutes or until vegetables are just crisp tender. Drain off water. Stir in margarine and salt and pepper to taste. Makes 4 servings.

Per serving:

CAL	PRO	CARB	FIB	FAT	SAT	CHOL	SOD
67	2g	13g	4g	1g	<1g	0mg	127mg

EASY CARROTS

TOP OF STOVE

1 1/2 pounds carrots
2 teaspoons soft tub margarine
1/2 cup chicken broth
Salt and pepper to taste

Peel carrots; slice diagonally into 1/4-inch slices. Melt margarine in medium saucepan. Add carrots and broth. Bring to a boil; reduce heat. Cover; simmer 10 minutes. Uncover; cook about 5 minutes or until carrots are crisp tender. Drain; toss with salt and pepper to taste. Makes 4 servings.

Per serving:

CAL	PRO	CARB	FIB	FAT	SAT	CHOL	SOD
98	2g	18g	6g	2g	<1g	0mg	306mg

FRESH ENGLISH PEAS

TOP OF STOVE

1/2 cup chicken broth
1 teaspoon soft tub margarine
2 cups shelled fresh English peas

Put chicken broth and margarine in small saucepan; bring to a boil. Add peas. Bring to a boil. Cook over medium heat 5 to 6 minutes or until peas are just crisp tender. Drain and serve. Makes four 1/2-cup servings.

Per serving:

CAL	PRO	CARB	FIB	FAT	SAT	CHOL	SOD
71	4g	11g	4g	1g	<1g	0g	136g

PEAS WITH WATER CHESTNUTS

TOP OF STOVE

6 tablespoons chicken broth
1/3 cup thin sliced red onion, about 4 slices, separated into rings
1 (10-ounce) package frozen peas
1/4 cup sliced water chestnuts (if too large, cut in half)
Dash pepper

In small saucepan, bring chicken broth to a boil. Add onion; cook about 2 minutes (they should still be crisp). Separate peas if necessary; add to onion along with water chestnuts. Cover; cook over medium heat until peas are heated through, but not soft. Add pepper to taste. Makes 4 servings.

Per serving:

CAL	PRO	CARB	FIB	FAT	SAT	CHOL	SOD
68	4g	13g	4g	<1g	<1g	0mg	110mg

BAKED PEAS

OVEN 350°

1 (10-ounce) package frozen peas
1/2 (8-ounce) can sliced water chestnuts, drained
1 teaspoon sugar
1/4 teaspoon salt
1/8 teaspoon ground pepper
1 tablespoon soft tub margarine

Place peas in 1-quart baking dish sprayed with vegetable cooking spray. Top with water chestnuts. Sprinkle with sugar, salt and pepper. Dot with small pieces of margarine. Cover; bake at 350° for 30 minutes or until heated through. Makes 4 servings.

Per serving:

CAL	PRO	CARB	FIB	FAT	SAT	CHOL	SOD
99	4g	15g	4g	3g	<1g	0mg	221mg

PEA PODS WITH PINEAPPLE

TOP OF STOVE

A colorful vegetable to serve with roast chicken and a rice dish.

2 tablespoons firmly packed light brown sugar
2 teaspoons cornstarch
2 tablespoons white vinegar
1 tablespoon reduced sodium soy sauce
1 (8-ounce) can pineapple chunks, reserve juice
3 cups fresh pea pods

Place brown sugar and cornstarch in medium saucepan; stir to mix well. Stir in vinegar, soy sauce and juice from pineapple. Cook, over medium heat, stirring frequently, until mixture comes to a boil. Add pineapple and pea pods. Cook until pea pods are crisp tender, about 8 to 10 minutes. Makes 4 servings.

VARIATION: Add 1/2 cup sliced water chestnuts.

Per serving:

CAL	PRO	CARB	FIB	FAT	SAT	CHOL	SOD
140	4g	28g	4g	<1g	<1g	0mg	129mg

THREE PEPPER STIR-FRY

TOP OF STOVE

This colorful vegetable stir-fry compliments almost any main course. Also makes a nice topping for pizza.

1 medium green pepper, sliced into rings
1 medium red pepper, sliced into rings
1 medium yellow pepper, sliced into rings
1 medium onion, sliced, separated into rings
1 1/2 teaspoons olive oil
Salt and pepper to taste

Heat olive oil in large non-stick skillet. Add vegetables; cook over medium heat until vegetables are crisp-tender, stirring occasionally. If desired, season to taste with salt and pepper. Makes 6 servings.

TIP: Because there is very little oil used, I often cover the skillet during part of the cooking time to prevent sticking. Size of recipe can be adjusted easily by using smaller or larger vegetables.

Per serving:

CAL	PRO	CARB	FIB	FAT	SAT	CHOL	SOD
38	<1g	6g	1g	1g	<1g	0mg	38mg

POTATOES WITH LEMON SAUCE

TOP OF STOVE

If desired, use small new red potatoes and steam until tender. Cut in half and pour sauce over; toss gently to coat.

2 pounds medium potatoes, peeled and quartered
2 tablespoons soft tub margarine
Juice of one lemon
3 tablespoons chopped green onion
Freshly ground black pepper
Dash of nutmeg

Cook potatoes in boiling water until just tender. Do not overcook or you will have mashed potatoes. Drain; cover to keep hot while combining remaining ingredients in a small saucepan. Heat until margarine is melted; stirring to blend. Put potatoes in serving dish. Pour sauce over top; gently toss to coat. Makes 6 servings.

Per serving:

CAL	PRO	CARB	FIB	FAT	SAT	CHOL	SOD
167	3g	31g	2g	4g	<1g	0mg	40mg

LIGHT CHEESY POTATOES

TOP OF STOVE
OVEN 350°

If you don't have a cup of mock sour cream made from nonfat yogurt in your refrigerator, you will need to start this recipe a day ahead. *See page 186.*

2 pounds potatoes, cooked until tender, cool
1 1/2 cups (6-ounces) Lite Mozzarella cheese, shredded
1/3 cup finely chopped onion
Salt and pepper to taste
1 cup mock sour cream
1/2 cup Lite sour cream

Peel potatoes and shred. Place in large mixing bowl. Lightly stir in shredded cheese and onion. Add salt and pepper. Combine the two sour creams. Fold into potato mixture. Spoon into 11 x 7-inch baking dish sprayed with vegetable cooking spray. The mixture will be quite thick; you will need to spread it evenly. Bake at 350° (325° if using glass) for about 1 hour 15 minutes, covering last 15 minutes with foil to prevent overbrowning. Makes 8 servings.

Per serving:

CAL	PRO	CARB	FIB	FAT	SAT	CHOL	SOD
181	13g	27g	2g	3g	3g	13mg	167mg

COMPANY ROASTED POTATOES

OVEN 425°

Per serving:

1 medium potato for baking
1 teaspoon soft tub margarine, melted
Salt
Paprika

Peel potatoes. Place on a cutting board and slice thinly (less than 1/4-inch) cutting almost to the bottom of potato, but not cutting through. Place in baking dish. Pour margarine over top; sprinkle lightly with paprika. Bake at 425° about 60 minutes or until potatoes are cooked through, basting a couple of times. Makes one serving.

Per serving:

CAL	PRO	CARB	FIB	FAT	SAT	CHOL	SOD
172	3g	34g	2g	3g	<1g	0mg	246mg

STUFFED POTATOES

OVEN 450°

A low cal version of twice baked potatoes. Can make ahead and heat just before serving. Delicious!

2 medium large baking potatoes
2 tablespoons soft tub margarine
2 tablespoons Lite sour cream
1/4 teaspoon dried dill weed
4 tablespoons nonfat milk
Salt and pepper to taste

Scrub potatoes. Prick all over with fork. Place on oven rack; bake at 450° for 50 to 60 minutes or until cooked through. Remove from oven. Cut in half lengthwise. Carefully scoop out potato, leaving a 1/4-inch shell. Place scooped out potato in small mixing bowl; add margarine, sour cream and dill weed. Beat until smooth, adding milk to thin (it may be necessary to use more or less milk, according to how thick the potato mixture is). Add salt and pepper to taste. Pile filling into potato shells. Reduce oven to 350°; bake potatoes about 8 to 10 minutes or until heated through. Makes 4 servings.

VARIATION: If desired, garnish top of each potato shell with a teaspoon of cooked crumbled bacon, a few cooked green peas or a sprinkle of paprika, parsley or grated Parmesan cheese.

Per serving:

CAL	PRO	CARB	FIB	FAT	SAT	CHOL	SOD
139	3g	18g	1g	6g	2g	3mg	118mg

STOVE TOP POTATOES WITH PEPPERS

TOP OF STOVE

A colorful and tasty vegetable dish.

2 teaspoons soft tub margarine
1 garlic clove, minced
1 pound small red potatoes, quartered (do not peel)
Salt and pepper to taste
1 medium green pepper, cut into narrow strips
1 medium red pepper, cut into narrow strips

Heat margarine in medium non-stick skillet. Add minced garlic; sauté about 1 minute. Add potatoes. Sprinkle with salt and pepper. Toss to coat. Cover; cook over low heat for 10 minutes. Add peppers; stir to mix. Cover and cook 5 to 10 minutes or until potatoes are just tender. Makes 4 servings.

Per serving:

CAL	PRO	CARB	FIB	FAT	SAT	CHOL	SOD
153	3g	32g	3g	2g	<1g	0mg	133mg

BAKED YAMS

OVEN 350°

Yams are sweet and have so much flavor, I don't think you need to put anything on them.

Per serving:

1 medium yam

Wash yam(s); place on rack in 350° oven. Bake 45 to 60 minutes or until cooked through.

Per yam:

CAL	PRO	CARB	FIB	FAT	SAT	CHOL	SOD
158	2	38g	na	<1g	<1g	0mg	11mg

APRICOT NUT RICE

TOP OF STOVE

A nice blend of flavors.

1 tablespoon soft tub margarine
1 cup finely chopped onion
1 cup uncooked long-grain rice
$2^1/_2$ cups chicken broth
$^1/_4$ cup finely chopped dried apricots
$^1/_4$ cup ($1^1/_4$-ounces) cashews, coarsely chopped

Melt margarine in medium saucepan. Add onions; sauté until soft. Add rice and chicken broth. Bring to a boil. Lower heat; cover and simmer 10 minutes. Stir in apricots and cashews. Cover and cook 8 to 10 minutes or until liquid is absorbed and rice is tender. Makes 6 servings.

Per serving:

CAL	PRO	CARB	FIB	FAT	SAT	CHOL	SOD
222	5g	37g	2g	6g	<1g	0mg	471mg

BAKED BROWN RICE

TOP OF STOVE
OVEN 350°

A delicious nutty flavor.

$^1/_4$ cup finely chopped onion
1 cup uncooked brown rice
$2^1/_4$ cups chicken broth
$^1/_2$ teaspoon mixed herbs

Sauté onion in small non-stick skillet sprayed with vegetable cooking spray cooking until soft. Stir in rice; cook until rice is heated through. Add chicken broth; bring to a boil. Pour into $1^1/_2$-quart baking dish sprayed with vegetable cooking spray. Cover; bake at 350° for 50 to 60 minutes or until liquid is absorbed and rice is tender. Makes 4 servings.

Per serving:

CAL	PRO	CARB	FIB	FAT	SAT	CHOL	SOD
185	5g	36g	3g	3g	<1g	0mg	568mg

LEMON VERMICELLI RICE

TOP OF STOVE

A nice blend of flavors and a great accompaniment to almost any dish.

2 teaspoons soft tub margarine
1/2 cup uncooked long-grain rice
1/2 cup vermicelli noodles, broken into 1-inch pieces
1 (14 1/2-ounces) can regular strength chicken broth
2 teaspoons grated lemon peel
1 teaspoon dried parsley

Melt margarine in medium saucepan. Add rice and vermicelli; sauté until light golden. Add broth, grated lemon peel and parsley; bring to a boil. Cover; reduce heat. Simmer about 15 minutes or until liquid is absorbed and rice is tender. Makes 4 servings.

Per serving:

CAL	PRO	CARB	FIB	FAT	SAT	CHOL	SOD
173	5g	31g	<1g	3g	<1g	0mg	469mg

Cook's Tip

Corn on the cob can be quickly cooked in the microwave oven. Wrap each ear of corn in a paper towel to completely enclose. Microwave on HIGH:

1 ear	-	*3 to 4 minutes*
2 ears	-	*5 to 6 minutes*
4 ears	-	*9 to 10 minutes*

PECAN-RICE PILAF

TOP OF STOVE

2 teaspoons soft tub margarine, divided
1/4 cup finely chopped pecans
1/3 cup finely chopped onion
1 cup uncooked long-grain rice
2 cups chicken broth
1/2 teaspoon salt

In medium saucepan, melt 1 teaspoon of the margarine. Sauté pecans to lightly toast. Remove and reserve. Add remaining margarine; sauté onions until slightly soft. Stir in rice. Add broth and salt. Bring to a boil; reduce heat. Cover; cook 15 to 20 minutes or until liquid is absorbed and rice is tender. Gently stir in pecans. Makes 6 servings.

Per serving:

CAL	PRO	CARB	FIB	FAT	SAT	CHOL	SOD
190	4g	31g	<1g	6g	<1g	0mg	523mg

RICE PILAF

TOP OF STOVE

A good company dish especially with chicken or beef.

1 tablespoon soft tub margarine
3/4 cup chopped onion
1 cup uncooked long-grain rice
2 cups chicken broth
1/2 teaspoon salt
1/4 teaspoon dried oregano

Melt margarine in medium saucepan. Add onion; cook until soft. Add rice; cook until rice is heated through, stirring often. Add remaining ingredients. Bring to a boil. Cover; lower heat; cook about 20 minutes or until liquid is absorbed and rice is tender. Makes 6 servings.

Per serving:

CAL	PRO	CARB	FIB	FAT	SAT	CHOL	SOD
303	7g	61g	1g	3g	<1g	0mg	530mg

RICE WITH PINEAPPLE

TOP OF STOVE

Rice goes with almost everything.

3 cups cooked long-grain rice (hot)
1/4 teaspoon salt
1/4 cup slivered almonds, toasted
1/3 cup pineapple juice, heated
1/2 cup pineapple tidbits
1 tablespoon soft tub margarine, melted

In medium saucepan combine all the ingredients; stir gently to mix. Cover; keep warm until ready to serve. Makes 4 servings.

Per serving:

CAL	PRO	CARB	FIB	FAT	SAT	CHOL	SOD
310	6g	54g	2g	8g	1g	0mg	162mg

VEGETABLE RICE DISH

TOP OF STOVE

This is one way to get more vegetables into your diet.

2 cups chicken broth
3/4 cup uncooked long-grain rice
1/4 cup finely chopped onion
1/4 cup chopped celery
1/2 cup shredded carrots
1/2 cup frozen peas

In medium saucepan, bring broth to a boil. Stir in remaining ingredients except peas. Cover; reduce heat and simmer about 18 minutes or until most of the liquid is absorbed. Stir in peas; cover and cook 2 to 3 minutes or until liquid is absorbed. Makes six 1/2-cup servings.

Per serving:

CAL	PRO	CARB	FIB	FAT	SAT	CHOL	SOD
131	4g	27g	2g	1g	<1g	0mg	360mg

Orange Couscous

Top of Stove

Couscous is a Moroccan pasta made from semolina. It takes only 5 minutes to cook, contains no fat and is very low in sodium.

1/3 cup green onions, thinly sliced on the bias
1 to 2 oranges (1/2 cup juice and 1 teaspoon grated peel)
1 cup chicken broth
1 teaspoon soft tub margarine
1 cup couscous

Combine onions, the 1/2 cup juice, orange peel, broth and margarine in medium saucepan. Bring to a boil; stir in couscous. Remove from heat. Cover and let stand 5 minutes. Makes 4 servings.

Per serving:

Cal	Pro	Carb	Fib	Fat	Sat	Chol	Sod
64	2g	11g	<1g	2g	<1g	0mg	261mg

Chinese Pasta Stir-Fry

Top of Stove

A colorful vegetable dish. For variation use frozen pea pods with water chestnuts.

6 ounces uncooked mostaccioli macaroni
1 teaspoon Canola oil
1 garlic clove, minced
1 (6-ounce) package frozen Chinese pea pods, thawed
1 medium red or yellow bell pepper, cut into narrow strips
Salt and pepper to taste

Cook mostaccioli according to directions on package; drain. Meanwhile, heat oil in large non-stick skillet. Add garlic, pea pods and pepper strips. Quickly cook vegetables, stirring frequently, until just crisp tender. Add noodles; salt and pepper to taste. Cook until heated through, watching carefully so as not to brown the noodles. Makes 6 servings.

Per serving:

Cal	Pro	Carb	Fib	Fat	Sat	Chol	Sod
156	6g	20g	1g	1g	<1g	0mg	37mg

ORZO PASTA PILAF

TOP OF STOVE

1 cup uncooked orzo pasta
1 cup frozen peas
3/4 cup finely chopped carrots
1 tablespoon soft tub margarine
1/4 teaspoon salt
1/4 cup grated Parmesan cheese

In large pot, bring 2 1/2 quarts water to a boil. Add orzo, peas and carrots. Continue to boil, 10 to 12 minutes or until pasta is cooked and vegetables are tender. Drain thoroughly. Place in large mixing bowl; toss with remaining ingredients. Makes 8 to 10 servings.

TIP: If more flavor is desired, cook in a well-seasoned chicken broth.

Per serving:

CAL	PRO	CARB	FIB	FAT	SAT	CHOL	SOD
148	6g	24g	2g	3g	<1g	3mg	171mg

VEGETABLE LASAGNA

TOP OF STOVE
OVEN 350°

The cheese should take the place of meat for this meal.

9 lasagna noodles
1 1/2 cups shredded carrots
1 cup coarsely chopped onion
1 red pepper, cut into narrow strips
2 cups broccoli flowerettes, cooked crisp tender
16 ounces Lite Mozzarella cheese, shredded

Cook noodles according to package directions. Meanwhile, place carrots, onion and pepper in medium non-stick skillet. Add 1/4 cup water. Cover; cook until vegetables are just tender. Remove from heat; stir in broccoli. Lightly spray 9 x 13-inch baking dish with vegetable cooking spray. Place 4 noodles in dish, overlapping slightly. Top with half the vegetable mixture. Sprinkle with a little over half the cheese. Repeat layers (the 9th noodle is for filling in any open spaces from broken or torn noodles). Bake at 350° (325° if using glass) for 30 minutes. Makes 8 servings.

TIP: If you want to cut the fat content further, decrease cheese to 12 ounces.

Per serving:

CAL	PRO	CARB	FIB	FAT	SAT	CHOL	SOD
276	24g	34g	3g	5g	4g	16mg	314mg

OIL-FREE CHILLED VEGETABLES

CHILL

This makes a great snack or vegetable with your meal. I like to serve it on top of a bed of assorted lettuce leaves. For additional color, add a few red pepper strips.

3/4 cup cider vinegar
1 cup sugar
1/2 pound cooked fresh green beans or 1 (16-ounce) can, drained
2 medium carrots cut into 1/4-inch strips
2 medium onions, sliced thin, separated into rings
Salt and fresh ground black pepper to taste (optional)

In large mixing bowl, combine vinegar and sugar. Stir in remaining ingredients. Cover tightly; chill several hours or overnight, turning bowl over or stirring vegetables occasionally to marinate. Makes 6 cups.

Per serving:

CAL	PRO	CARB	FIB	FAT	SAT	CHOL	SOD
181	2g	46g	3g	<1g	<1g	0mg	12mg

SAUTÉED VEGETABLES

TOP OF STOVE

1 tablespoon soft tub margarine (or olive oil)
2 medium onions, cut into thin wedges and separated
1/2 pound fresh mushrooms, sliced
1 medium green pepper, cut into narrow strips
3 tablespoons dry sherry
1/2 teaspoon salt (optional)

Melt margarine in large non-stick skillet. Add vegetables; toss to mix. Add sherry. Cook over medium heat until vegetables are just crisp tender. Sprinkle with salt if desired. A great accompaniment to steak. Makes 8 servings.

Per serving:

CAL	PRO	CARB	FIB	FAT	SAT	CHOL	SOD
58	2g	9g	2g	2g	<1g	0mg	15mg

STEAMED VEGETABLE MIX

TOP OF STOVE

2 carrots, sliced in 1/4-inch slices
1 onion, cut into wedges, separated
1 medium red pepper, cut into narrow strips
1 medium small zucchini, sliced
2 teaspoons soft tub margarine
Salt and pepper to taste

Place carrots, onion and red pepper in large steamer basket. Place over boiling water; cover and cook 6 minutes. Add zucchini; continue cooking 3 to 4 minutes or until vegetables are just crisp tender. Place in large serving bowl; gently toss with margarine. Sprinkle with salt and pepper. Makes 4 servings.

Per serving:

CAL	PRO	CARB	FIB	FAT	SAT	CHOL	SOD
70	2g	12g	4g	2g	<1g	0mg	125mg

ONION SPAGHETTI DINNER

TOP OF STOVE

A good pasta dish for days when you choose not to have meat with your meal. Makes a lot.

3 medium onions, sliced thin, separated into rings
1 tablespoon olive oil
1/4 cup dry sherry
1/2 cup plus 8 teaspoons grated Parmesan, divided
1 (16-ounce) package spaghetti
1 (30-ounce) jar extra chunky spaghetti sauce with mushrooms

In large skillet, cook onion in oil, covered, about 20 minutes or until onions are just beginning to soften. Add sherry; cook, uncovered, until liquid has evaporated. Meanwhile cook the spaghetti as directed on package. Drain; combine with onions. Stir in the 1/2 cup Parmesan. Meanwhile heat spaghetti sauce. Serve 1/2 cup sauce over each serving of noodles. Sprinkle with 1 teaspoon Parmesan. Makes 8 servings.

Per servng:

CAL	PRO	CARB	FIB	FAT	SAT	CHOL	SOD
454	14g	74g	1g	10g	2g	6mg	631mg

STEAMED CABBAGE

TOP OF STOVE

1 pound raw cabbage
1/2 teaspoon salt
1 tablespoon soft tub margarine
1 cup water
White pepper

Cut cabbage into bite-size pieces. In large saucepan, add salt, margarine and water. Bring to a simmer; add cabbage. Cover; cook 6 to 8 minutes or until cabbage is crisp tender (do not overcook). Drain. Season with pepper. Makes 4 servings.

TIP: If you have some leftover ham, add about 1/4 cup cut into small cubes.

Per serving:

CAL	PRO	CARB	FIB	FAT	SAT	CHOL	SOD
36	1g	5g	3g	2g	<1g	0mg	167mg

SALSA

CHILL

Make day ahead to allow flavors to blend.

3 cups diced ripe, but firm tomatoes
1 (4-ounce) can green chilies
1/4 cup finely chopped onion
1 tablespoon olive oil
1 teaspoon cider vinegar
3/4 teaspoon salt

Combine ingredients until well mixed. Chill overnight to blend flavors. Makes 3 1/2 cups.

TIP: If more color is desired, substitute sliced green onions for the chopped onion.

Per serving (1 tablespoon):

CAL	PRO	CARB	FIB	FAT	SAT	CHOL	SOD
5	<1g	<1g	<1g	<1g	0g	0mg	30mg

Index

Great Meals Begin with Six Ingredients Or Less

Six Ingredients Or Less Cookbook - over 500 recipes from everyday cooking to delicious company entertaining. Sections include: Appetizers, Breads, Cookies, Desserts, Beef, Poultry, Vegetables and many more.

Six Ingredients Or Less Chicken Cookbook - dedicated to a familiar and favorite standby, from appetizers, salads, and main dishes to 20 complete menus for plan-ahead dining.

Six Ingredients Or Less Light & Healthy - great cooking your family will love, and they'll never know the recipes are good for them. Recipes include nutritional analysis for calories, fat grams, cholesterol, sodium, etc.

If you cannot find our **Six Ingredients Or Less Cookbooks** at your local store, order directly from C.J. Books. Copy or fill out the order blank below and return, with your check or money order to:

SIX INGREDIENTS OR LESS
P.O. Box 922
Gig Harbor, WA 98335
206-851-3778

Remember, Cookbooks Make Great Gifts!

(Birthdays, Christmas, Mother's Day, Weddings, Showers, House warmings, Thank yous, Campers, Boaters)

Six Ingredients Or Less	(_____# of copies)	$10.95 each	$_______
Six Ingredients Or Less Chicken Cookbook	(_____# of copies)	$10.95 each	$_______
Six Ingredients Or Less Light & Healthy	(_____# of copies)	$10.95 each	$_______
Plus postage & handling		$1.25 **each**	$_______
Subtotal			$_______
Washington residents add sales tax		.95 **each**	$_______
Total			**$_______**

Please Print or Type

(please double-check addition, differences will be billed)

NAME ____

ADDRESS ____

CITY____________________________STATE_______ZIP ______________

GREAT MEALS BEGIN WITH SIX INGREDIENTS OR LESS®

Six Ingredients Or Less Cookbook - over 500 recipes from everyday cooking to delicious company entertaining. Sections include: Appetizers, Breads, Cookies, Desserts, Beef, Poultry, Vegetables and many more.

Six Ingredients Or Less Chicken Cookbook - dedicated to a familiar and favorite standby, from appetizers, salads, and main dishes to 20 complete menus for plan-ahead dining.

Six Ingredients Or Less Light & Healthy - great cooking your family will love, and they'll never know the recipes are good for them. Recipes include nutritional analysis for calories, fat grams, cholesterol, sodium, etc.

Six Ingredients Or Less Pasta & Casseroles - the perfect answer to today's hectic lifestyles. Original and lowfat version for each recipe, including nutritional analysis.

If you cannot find our **Six Ingredients Or Less Cookbooks** at your local store, order directly from C.J. Books. Copy or fill out the order blank below and return, with your check or money order to:

SIX INGREDIENTS OR LESS®
P.O. BOX 922
GIG HARBOR, WA 98335
***OR CALL* 1-800-423-7184**

Remember, Cookbooks Make Great Gifts!

Six Ingredients Or Less	(_____# of copies)	$12.95 each	$_______
Six Ingredients Or Less Chicken Cookbook	(_____# of copies)	$12.95 each	$_______
Six Ingredients Or Less Light & Healthy	(_____# of copies)	$12.95 each	$_______
Six Ingredients Or Less Pasta & Casseroles	(_____# of copies)	$14.95 each	$_______
Plus Postage & Handling: First Book $1.75. Additional books, add $ 1.00 each.			$_______
Subtotal			$_______
Washington residents add sales tax - 7.9%			$_______
Total			**$**_______

PLEASE PRINT OR TYPE

(please double-check addition, differences will be billed)

____ **VISA** Card # ______________________________

____ **MasterCard** Exp.Date _____ Signature ______________________

NAME____

ADDRESS ____

CITY_________________________STATE______ZIP____________